aPHR Study Guide

2023–2024

360 Test Questions and Detailed Answer Explanations for the Associate Professional in Human Resources Certification

Table of Contents

Introduction

The Associate Professional in Human Resources (aPHR) Exam is a certification administered by the HR Certification Institute (HRCI).

It is intended for individuals beginning their HR career or those who have worked in HR for a short period of time and want to establish their credibility and demonstrate their commitment to the HR profession.

The exam consists of 100 multiple-choice questions, and test-takers have two hours to complete it. To be eligible to take the aPHR exam, candidates must have a high school diploma or equivalent.

There are five functional areas tested in the computer-based exam:

1 – Talent Acquisition: Tests candidates' knowledge of recruitment, selection and onboarding of new intakes.

2 – Learning and Development: Tests candidates' knowledge of training and development.

3 – Compensation and Benefits: Tests candidates' knowledge of salary structures, annual benefits and incentive plans.

4 – Employee Relations: Tests candidates' knowledge of performance management, employee retention rate and engagement.

5 – Compliance and Risk Management: Tests candidates' knowledge of employment laws, data privacy and workplace safety.

Testing Rules

The rules and regulations surrounding the aPHR exam are strict and include the following:

- Candidates are not allowed to take breaks during the two-hour test session.
- Candidates cannot take extra materials like calculators, notes or cell phones into the testing area.
- If candidates exit the testing center for any reason, they will not be allowed to resume the exam.
- The allocated time is for both attempting and reviewing the test questions.
- All candidates must bring identification documents to the testing center.
- Any distracting behavior will not be tolerated.
- Wearing smartwatches or bringing any electronic device to the exam is strictly prohibited.
- Communicating with other candidates during the exam is not allowed.

How to Register for the Exam

To register for the exam, follow these steps:

1. Log on to the HRCI official website.

2. Create an account.

3. Select your desired testing site and complete the payment and registration fees.

Where to Take the Test

The aPHR test is administered at approved test centers in 125 countries. Candidates can look for the nearest test center on the HRCI website during registration.

Guidelines for Conduct During the aPHR Exam

Candidates must follow the following guidelines during the aPHR exam:

- Follow the instructions provided by the testing center's staff.
- Only use the writing material provided by the staff.
- Answer questions to the best of one's knowledge.

- Review or make changes to questions within the allotted time.

Section 1 - Talent Acquisition

Chapter 1: Fundamentals of Human Resource Management (HRM)

Human resource management (HRM) is a term that refers to the strategies, practices and processes used by organizations to coordinate, organize and manage employee onboarding, retention and training.

Essentially, HRM is related to the employment relationship between an organization and its employees.

In this chapter, we will examine the aspects of HRM and understand how HR managers provide benefits to companies and organizations.

Responsibilities of HR

The responsibilities of HR can vary depending on the company's size, workforce and complexity. In general, the department has a few basic responsibilities, most of which are mentioned below:

Talent Acquisition: HR has to oversee talent-hunting processes, such as creating job descriptions, conducting market analyses to figure out competitive salaries and managing interviews and onboarding.

Running Compensation Programs: HR manages employee affairs and compensation programs, including gross salary, health insurance, retirement plans and bonuses.

Managing Employees: HR has to mediate and resolve difficulties and challenges faced by employees, such as work investigations, performance issues and disagreements.

Conducting Performance Evaluations: HR must make sure company employees are meeting targets. They do this by conducting performance evaluations that take an in-depth look into employee productivity and provide feedback.

Ensuring Compliance: Companies have to adhere to tax and employment laws like the ADA and FLSA. They could face penalties and fines if they don't. HR makes sure they comply with employment laws.

Aside from the responsibilities above, HR may also have to ensure and enforce talent management, diversity and inclusion and employee communications in larger companies.

The size and structure of the HR department can vary with the organization's size, with larger companies often having much more specialized roles and a more complex structure.

The HR department is crucial to achieving the organization's goals and objectives by recruiting, keeping and growing qualified staff.

The HR department contributes to an engaged and productive staff by establishing a good work environment, offering competitive remuneration and benefits and ensuring compliance with relevant laws and regulations.

Factors Impacting HRM: Internal and External

HRM is driven by internal and external variables. Understanding these factors is critical for firms to properly manage their staff and achieve their objectives.

Internal factors impacting work culture include:

Organizational Culture

An organization's culture substantially impacts HRM practices since it influences employee attitudes, behaviors and values.

A positive company culture may promote employee engagement and satisfaction, whereas a toxic culture can result in high turnover and low morale.

Management Style

Managers' and supervisors' leadership styles substantially influence HRM practices since they affect employee motivation and work satisfaction.

A supportive and participatory management style can result in high levels of employee engagement, whereas an authoritarian approach can result in low morale and high turnover.

Employee Demographics

Workers' age, gender, education level and other demographic traits can influence HRM practices since they influence the sorts of perks and programs that employees may desire.

Organizational Structure

An organization's structure can influence HRM practices, as it impacts the extent of authority and decision-making ability of HR professionals.

A flat organizational structure, together with decentralized decision-making, might result in far more adaptable and responsive HR strategies. A hierarchical structure, however, can lead to strict and bureaucratic HR procedures.

External factors impacting work culture include:

Economic Factors

These factors, including inflation, recession and unemployment, can influence HRM practices because they affect job availability, employee demand and the cost of benefits and pay.

The Legal and Regulatory Environment

The legal and regulatory environment may have a considerable influence on HRM practices since it determines the sorts of benefits and programs that firms can provide and the restrictions they must follow.

Competition

As firms recruit and retain top talent, competition for outstanding individuals can influence HRM practices. This can lead to greater benefits and remuneration, as well as the creation of new HR initiatives and procedures.

Technological Improvements

Technological improvements can influence HRM practices since they change how firms manage and interact with their personnel. For instance, the increased usage of social media, as well as online platforms, can have an impact on recruiting and communication techniques.

Types of Employee Classification

The process of categorizing employees based on criteria like tasks, experience, abilities and duties is referred to as employee categorization.

Organizations are able to make use of employee categorization to help them keep tabs on their workers, make informed choices regarding pay, benefits and promotions, and remain in compliance with labor laws as well as regulations.

Firms must regularly review and upgrade their employee categorization systems to make sure that they accurately reflect the changing requirements as well as expectations of the business and its employees.

A few of the most prevalent types of employee classification are discussed below:

Part Time vs. Full Time: This depends on the number of hours an individual works every week. This impacts the benefits employees receive as well as the time off they get.

Permanent vs. Temporary: This is based on the length of employment. It determines the benefits employees receive as well as their job security.

Salaried vs. Hourly: This determines whether workers are paid by the hour or as a prenegotiated flat cost.

Entry-level vs. Experienced Professional: The experience level of employees determines the general stage of their career.

Differences Between HRM vs. Personnel Management

HRM, as well as personnel management (PM), are similar terms used for describing the management of employees in a company. Even though the two terms are used interchangeably, there are a few important differences.

PM is a standard method of employee oversight, which concentrates on operations such as payroll, benefits administration and compliance with labor laws. It focuses mainly on guaranteeing stability and reducing risk.

HRM is a more strategic and proactive approach to managing workers. It focuses on creating and applying policies and programs which help attain the organization's vision and mission. HRM is centered on identifying, retaining and developing talent, in addition to boosting employee engagement and work satisfaction.

The focus of each approach is also a crucial distinction between the two terms. HRM centers around attaining strategic objectives and enhancing organizational performance, while PM is mainly focused on ensuring balance and reducing risk.

Types of HR Strategies

HR strategies are the strategies and techniques that businesses implement to train and manage their workers and achieve their objectives. There are three fundamental types of HR strategies:

Corporate: The corporate HR approach seeks to align a company's HR procedures with its overall company strategy. It ensures that the HR procedures, as well as applications of the organization, conform with its vision and mission and align with its core values.

Competitive: The competitive HR approach focuses on the differences between the company's practices and its competition. It's committed to attracting, developing and retaining top talent while offering a comprehensive pay and benefits package that is both attractive and competitive.

Functional: The functional HR strategy enhances particular HR capabilities like recruitment, development and training, salary and benefits and employment relations. It aims to enhance the effectiveness as well as the efficiency of these functions and to make sure they conform to the company's vision and core values.

Chapter 2: Workforce Planning and Talent Sourcing

Workforce or HR planning is a process that allows HR to understand the current and future needs of the workforce in an organization. It helps organizations accomplish their mission, goals and strategic plans by employing the right number of people.

Most organizations, especially corporations, may have workforce planning teams, while others may only use the process when going through a merger, acquisition or similar situations. Here's what the workforce planning process entails:

Assessing the Current HR Situation: This entails a comprehensive evaluation of the present HR situation inside the organization, including employee turnover and ability shortages, as well as the availability of workers.

Forecasting Future HR Needs: HR managers make use of forecasting methods to determine the quality and quantity of talent needed, depending on the company's business plans and goals.

Creating HR Strategies: Based on the expected HR requirements, HR professionals create strategies for recruiting and retention to meet the company's future needs.

Executing Plans: When HR strategies are created, HR professionals collaborate with various departments in the organization to execute the plans and make sure the company has solutions established for execution.

Monitoring and Evaluating Changes: HR professionals monitor and assess the HR planning process and make changes as needed to ensure the business will continue to fulfill its HR demands and goals.

Dimensions of an HR Plan

An effective HR plan must have a number of crucial dimensions to make sure that a company is properly covering its HRs needs. It needs to have the following dimensions:

Workforce Analysis: This is the first step of HR planning and entails assessing the situation inside the business, including aspects such as employee turnover, ability gaps and staffing levels. This analysis provides the basis for anticipating future HR requirements.

Forecasting the Workforce: This entails utilizing data and analytics to determine the types of workers a company will need down the road. It helps to determine any possible gaps between the present HR capacities of the organization and its future HR needs.

Talent Acquisition Strategy: This identifies the steps an organization should take to locate, recruit and hire personnel. These include creating job descriptions, determining the sources of talent and developing an efficient recruiting process.

Types of HR Plans

Plan for Recruitment/Selection

A selection and recruitment plan is a document that identifies the steps which a company usually takes to identify, hire and retain new employees. The plan generally consists of information about the following elements:

Job Analysis and Description: A comprehensive description of the job tasks, duties and requirements of the job being filled.

List of Recruitment Sources: A listing of the numerous sources that will be utilized to employ new workers, including job boards, employee referrals and college recruiting functions.

The Screening Process: The steps which will be taken to select and assess candidates, including résumé reviews, telephone screenings and in-person interviews.

Assessment Methods: The techniques utilized to evaluate applicants consist of cognitive and behavioral assessments, ability tests and reference checks.

Selection Criteria: The criteria used in making ultimate hiring decisions are experience, education and cultural fit.

Timelines: A schedule that describes the different phases of the recruiting and selection processes as well as the time frame for each.

Budget: An estimation of the expenditures incurred in the hiring and selection process and assessment tools, including advertising and travel expenses.

Retention Plan

A retention plan describes the measures an organization will have to take to retain its employees and reduce high turnover and disengagement rates. The plan generally consists of information about the following elements:

Employee Engagement: Strategies for enhancing employee engagement, including providing a good work environment, offering career advancement opportunities and rewarding great overall performance.

Total Rewards: An overview of the company's total rewards program, including compensation, benefits and nonmonetary rewards to ensure the company is both appealing to workers and competitive.

Career Development: A strategy that provides workers with opportunities to improve their careers through training, development courses, mentoring and job rotations.

Balance of Work and Life: Flexibility in work schedules, paid time off, as well as health programs are some strategies for enhancing a company's work-life balance.

Communication: A strategy to enhance communication between workers as well as management, which includes regular employee surveys and town hall meetings.

Disposal Plan

A disposal plan is a document that explains the methods a company will follow to eliminate redundant or excess personnel. The plan generally consists of information about the following elements:

Redundancy Criteria: The criteria will be used to determine surplus or redundant employees based on factors including changes in business operations, declining product sales and cost-cutting measures.

Plan for Employee Consultation: A method of speaking with employees and their representatives to clarify the conditions of the redundancy and provide support throughout the transition.

Plan for Severance Pay: A program that offers severance pay along with other benefits to affected workers, including outplacement assistance, retraining courses and job search assistance.

Plan for Outplacement Support: A method for offering outplacement assistance to impacted workers, which includes career coaching, résumé writing assistance and job search assistance.

Forecast Staffing Needs

Forecasting staffing requirements is a crucial part of HR planning as it helps companies ensure they have the proper number of workers with the right skills and expertise to achieve their objectives.

The following are some steps to help you forecast staffing needs:

Examine Organizational Objectives and Goals

Begin by looking at your organization's goals and objectives, which include growth plans, new service or product launches and changes in market conditions. This will allow you to figure out the staffing needed to support these initiatives.

Analyze Current Staffing Levels

Examine your current staffing levels and take into consideration factors like employee turnover, retirement and promotions to identify any gaps in your current workforce and determine how much staff you will need to fill them.

Forecast Future Demand

Once you've understood your staffing needs, you should perform analyses to find out how many employees you will need in the future to meet the demand for your services.

Job Analysis: What is it?

When HR begins collecting and analyzing information that is specific to a job, this is considered a job analysis. It usually focuses on figuring out the job's requirements, responsibilities, skills, benefits and other details.

Job analyses typically contain three components:

Worker Attributes: Data on skills needed to perform the job.

Work Context: Data on the internal and external job environment.

Worker Activities: Data on the responsibilities of a job.

Job analyses help HR professionals hire the right employees for organizational positions.

Use Cases of Job Analysis

The information collected through job analysis may be utilized in a number of ways by organizations. A few of the key uses could be as follows:

Recruitment and Selection

Job analysis data can be utilized to produce detailed job descriptions, which are important for recruiting and selecting competent candidates. These descriptions are used by companies to figure out the knowledge, skills and capabilities needed for a specific organizational position.

HR also uses job descriptions to understand which candidates best fit the position.

Figuring Out the Appropriate Salary

By using job analysis information, HR departments can determine the right salary amount for every job they post. They do this by looking at factors such as the level of responsibility, knowledge, skills and experience necessary for the position.

How to Collect Job Analysis Information

A few techniques for gathering information for task analysis include:

Questionnaires

Questionnaires can be used to collect data about the job tasks, responsibilities, knowledge and skills needed for the position.

The questionnaire can be produced to collect both quantitative and qualitative data.

Observation

Observing employees while they perform their tasks offers useful awareness of the expertise, abilities and necessary skills needed to effectively finish the process at hand.

This method can help HR figure out the particular duties to be carried out, the program and tools utilized, and the amount of knowledge essential to finish the job.

Worker Sampling

Worker sampling entails observing an individual performing a job for a fixed time period. It is typically used to calculate the duration of time needed to finish the work, as well as the expertise required for the task.

The Crucial Incident Technique

This entails collecting information regarding particular incidents or events that have had an influence on the job. These incidents could be positive or negative and supply grounds for figuring out the expertise, abilities and skills needed to effectively perform the job.

Developing a Task Inventory

This involves producing a summary of tasks that a worker has done. The checklist might be utilized to figure out how many points are invested in every activity and the amount of knowledge required to finish the task, as well as how crucial the process was.

Functional Job Analysis (FJA)

FJA is a method that examines the mental, physical and informative facets of a job to figure out the expertise, abilities and capabilities needed for the project to be carried out effectively.

Document Review

The documentation review technique looks at associated papers, such as employment descriptions, general performance reviews and training materials to obtain data about the job.

Businesses are able to utilize a selection of techniques to get job analysis data. The most effective strategy will be based on the specific demands of the group, along with the information type needed.

Tips on Sourcing Internal Talent

Sourcing internal talent refers to getting workers within a company to fill a new or existing position. It's a helpful strategy for companies looking to develop a strong and competent workforce.

To obtain internal talent, companies may utilize some of the following strategies:

Determine Current Employee Skills and Competencies: The initial step in sourcing internal talent is to determine the abilities and competencies of present workers. This may be achieved via job descriptions, performance assessments or abilities evaluations.

Create a Succession Plan: Organizations are able to create a succession plan that determines high-potential workers with the ability to transfer into crucial positions in the long term. This can help make sure the company carries a pipeline of internal workers to fill essential roles as they start to become available.

Foster a Culture of Professional Development: By motivating personnel to create new skills and accept new challenges, companies are able to develop a culture of professional development that fosters internal talent.

Encourage Employee Mobility: Organizations are able to promote employee mobility by permitting employees to transfer between various roles or departments within the business. This can help create a diverse and adaptable workforce and provide workers with brand-new opportunities to improve their knowledge and skills.

Offer Development and Training Opportunities: Organizations are able to offer training and development opportunities to assist workers in developing the abilities and understanding they need to be successful in new positions. This may include on-the-job instruction, mentoring, coaching and more structured training courses.

Advertise From Within: By encouraging internal staff to apply to open positions, businesses are able to show their dedication to inner skill and produce a work environment that encourages motivation and engagement.

Tips on How You Can Source External Talent

Sourcing outside skills is the act of determining and appealing to job applicants from outside a business to fill up new or existing positions. Here are a few ways organizations can source external talent:

Build a Solid Employer Brand: A strong brand helps organizations attract prospective applicants to the business because of its culture, values and mission. This enables the organization to win over talent from outside the company.

Utilize Job Boards and Recruitment Sites: Organizations are able to make use of job boards and recruitment sites for advertising and marketing open jobs and appealing to prospective candidates. This helps companies reach a large pool of suitable candidates quickly and efficiently.

Networking Events and Host Career Fairs: Organizations are able to host career fairs and network events to meet up with prospects personally and exchange information on open positions and company culture.

Create Employee Referral Programs: Employee referral programs help organizations effectively source outside talent by using existing employees' personal connections and networks.

Work with Headhunters and Recruitment Agencies: Organizations can work with recruitment companies and headhunters to recruit top talent from outside the business.

Provide Competitive Benefits and Compensation Packages: Offering competitive compensation and benefits packages will assist in luring top talent from outside the business.

Techniques for Sourcing Talent

There are a number of techniques for obtaining talent. A few examples include:

Rehires and Transfers

Rehires and transfers tend to have two internal sources of employment. Rehires are past workers brought back to benefit the organization once again.

Rehiring is typically an inexpensive method of acquiring talent because the company has some awareness of the person's previous performance and of how it fits within the business culture.

On the other hand, transfer cases refer to personnel moving from one department to another. This is often a great way to obtain talent for new jobs within the company since the worker is already acquainted with the business culture and policies.

Furthermore, transferred personnel provide an abundance of experience and expertise in the brand-new position, making the change much easier for both the worker as well as the company.

Temp -to-Lease Programs

Temp-to-lease programs, also called temporary-to-permanent programs, are staffing solutions that allow companies to hire personnel temporarily, with the option to transform them into permanent workers later.

The major benefit of temp-to-perm applications is that they allow companies to assess an employee's abilities and performance inside the business culture prior to making a long-term commitment. This is especially helpful for companies aiming to fill crucial roles or roles needing specific skills.

In a temp-to-perm system, an employee works for a certain time, during which the company is able to assess performance and determine whether it wants to provide the person with a permanent job.

When the worker performs well and the company is pleased with the performance, it may then provide a permanent job, often at a higher salary. However, if the worker doesn't match the company's standards, the temporary agreement can be terminated with no obligation to give the person a permanent job.

Recruiting Through the Internet

Recruiting via the web makes use of Internet technologies to recruit and hire workers. The web has transformed how companies source and engage talent, supplying an extensive pool of applicants and enabling more cost-effective and effective recruitment processes.

Some typical ways of recruiting on the web include:

- Posting openings on job boards and organization sites to reach a wide pool of prospective employees.
- Utilizing social networking sites, including LinkedIn, Twitter and Facebook, to develop a talent pool.
- Allowing applicants to access employment vacancies online via business sites or web-based application systems.
- Conducting first interviews with prospective candidates through video-conferencing systems like Skype or Zoom.

- Utilizing AI and machine-learning algorithms to examine résumés, determine possible candidates and automate repetitive recruitment jobs.

College Recruiting

College recruiting describes the method of engaging and employing recent graduates and college students for part time or intern posts inside a company. It's generally a critical element of a company's talent acquisition method because it provides access to a pool of younger, driven and gifted individuals who can provide new ideas and perspectives on the business.

College recruiting generally entails on-campus recruiting functions, networking events, informational interviews and job fairs. Businesses can even utilize Internet recruiting programs, including social media, job boards and university career centers, to meet prospective applicants.

Referrals and Walk-ins

Employer referrals may be an invaluable source of talent since they're oftentimes from a trusted and reliable source.

Walk-ins occur when a person visits the company with no appointment, generally to ask about employment openings or to provide a résumé. Walk-ins can originate from a variety of sources, such as job fairs, career clinics or the organization's site.

Advertising

Advertising makes use of different media outlets to attract prospective candidates. It works to reach qualified talent and encourage them to apply.

Businesses may utilize specialized recruiting advertising, like professional associations or college newspapers, to reach certain target groups. Advertising can offer several benefits to companies, such as:

Wider Reach: Advertising reaches a diverse audience of potential applicants, boosting the odds of locating the best match.

Cost-effectiveness: Advertising can be a cost-effective method to reach possible applicants, particularly when compared with other recruitment techniques, including direct headhunting or sourcing.

Employment Agencies

Employment businesses, also called staffing agencies, assist organizations in locating and hiring workers. These companies provide a variety of services, such as payroll management, temporary staffing and job placement.

By utilizing an employment agency, companies are able to save time in the selection process by relying on the third-party company to filter and prequalify applicants, lowering the demand for in-house selection and recruitment tasks.

In some instances, utilizing an employment agency may be much more economical than in-house selection and recruitment activities because the company takes responsibility for most of the expenses related to the recruitment process, including marketing and background checks.

Phased Retirement

Phased retirement is a flexible working agreement that enables personnel to slowly move into retirement by lowering their working hours and duties over time.

It's a voluntary system that lets employees keep working in a decreased capacity while obtaining partial retirement benefits.

The gradual retirement process benefits both personnel and employers. For personnel, it allows the continuity of employment in a decreased capacity while also providing retirement benefits. For companies, it helps retain valuable experience and talent while offering opportunities for workers to transfer their expertise to the coming generation of employees.

Contractor Payrolling

Contractor payrolling, also referred to as "employer of record" or "payrolling services," is a method where a third-party organization can serve as the employer for employees or freelance workers.

The third-party organization handles the duties of securing the contractor's income and administering payroll taxes and benefits, along with any other HR-related tasks.

Contract payrolling is a well-known choice for companies that must fill project-based or short-term roles or maybe for those who wish to lessen the costs and duties related to hiring conventional workers.

Job Screening: Employee Testing and Simulations

Employee testing interviews screen job candidates through different assessments, tests and simulations to determine their suitability for a specific function.

Job selection is intended to determine the best applicants for a particular task based on their capabilities, knowledge and skills.

A variety of different kinds of employee testing and simulations are typically used in employment interviewing. Some examples include:

Skills Tests: These tests evaluate a candidate's performance for a project, including typing speed, computer programming and data entry.

Cognitive Ability Tests: These tests assess an individual's potential to research, process information and make choices. They frequently contain aptitude assessments, reasoning tests and intelligence tests.

Personality Tests: These tests assess an individual's attributes and preferences, including work style, inspiration and emotional intelligence.

Simulation Exercises: These exercises imitate real-job duties, permitting candidates to display their abilities and capabilities in a controlled setting.

What Are Work Samples?

Work samples involve asking candidates to complete a task representative of the work they would perform if hired.

For example, a candidate for a graphic design role might be asked to create an illustration as part of the interview process.

What Are Simulations?

Simulations are example scenarios that run candidates through a certain job's tasks and working conditions. They include computer-based simulations, role-playing exercises or job-based simulations.

For example, candidates applying for project management jobs could take part in job-based simulations to show their skills.

Advantages of Utilizing Simulations and Work Samples

There are advantages to utilizing work samples and simulations in the recruiting process.

Enhanced Accuracy: Simulations and work samples offer a far more accurate assessment of a prospect's skills and abilities compared to conventional interviews.

Objective Evaluation: Simulations and work samples impartially assess a person's overall performance, lowering the impact of individual biases and subjectiveness.

Increased Candidate Engagement: By doing work samples and participating in simulations, applicants can display their abilities and skills, making the recruiting process much more stimulating and inspiring.

What Are Management Assessment Centers?

Management assessment centers are usually a systematic assessment method utilized to evaluate the abilities and capabilities of supervisors and possible managers. The aim of management assessment centers is to establish a person's suitability for a management job and determine the individual's weaknesses and areas for growth. They truthfully assess a candidate's achievements, lowering the effect of individual biases and subjectiveness.

Usually, the tasks utilized in management assessment centers are made in order to mimic real management situations and to check certain competencies, like problem-solving, communication, leadership, decision-making and interpersonal skills.

Participants are generally offered performance criteria in advance so they understand what's anticipated from them.

How to Pick the Correct Job Screening Tool

Choosing the appropriate job screening device is an essential part of the hiring task since it helps to make sure you choose the appropriate person for the task.

The following are several crucial considerations while picking out a job screening tool:

Job Requirements: Think about the precise abilities, knowledge and expertise needed for the job when choosing a screening tool. For instance, a technical examination might be more suitable compared to a personality test if the job calls for technical knowledge.

Legal Considerations: Ensure that the screening tool complies with all relevant laws and regulations, such as antidiscrimination laws.

Validity and Reliability: Choose a validated screening tool with a demonstrated track record of accurately predicting job performance.

Time and Cost: Consider the expense and time needed for executing and scoring the screening tool, as well as the materials needed to teach people to utilize it.

Objectivity: Pick a screening tool that is free of individual biases and subjectivity.

Ease of Use: Choose a screening tool that is very easy to administer, score and understand and which provides actionable and clear results.

Customization: Think about the assessment tool and whether it can be personalized to meet your company's particular requirements.

What Are Background Investigations?

Background inquiries are usually detailed overviews of a person's past, carried out together with the selection process to make sure the applicant is ideal for the project.

A background check is designed to give a thorough and balanced evaluation of a candidate's past and present to assist the employer in making an informed hiring decision.

The extent of a background check may differ based on the dynamics of the job as well as the employer's needs; however, it generally incorporates the following elements:

Education Verification: Ensures the person has educational credentials outlined in their résumé.

Employment Verification: Establishes the applicant's work record and earlier job titles, duties and dates of employment.

Reference Checks: Telephone or in-person interviews with earlier coworkers and supervisors to get insight into the person's job performance, behavior and persona.

Credit Check: Validates the applicant's credit record and financial standing.

License Verification: Confirms the person has the required certifications or licenses necessary for the task.

Chapter 3: Talent Recruitment, HR Metrics and Data Collection

Talent recruitment and HR metrics are crucial aspects of HR management. Each has an essential role in ensuring a business attracts and retains the best skill.

Collecting data will be the basis of HR metrics since the information collected gives insights into the success of recruitment plus talent management methods.

Interviews: Beginning the Onboarding Process

Interviews are an important component of the onboarding activity since they help determine if a prospect is a great match for the job and the organization. They give both the employer and the applicant a chance to evaluate one another.

The job interview procedure assists the onboarding procedure by:

Verifying Information: Interviews are performed to confirm the details supplied by the applicant on the résumé and application.

Considering Abilities and Skills: The interviewer evaluates the individual's skills, capabilities and expertise and determines if the person is appropriate for the job.

Assessing Cultural Fit: Interviews may help assess the person's compatibility with the business culture and determine how the individual might fit the current staff.

Offering Data: The job interview may supply the person with additional details about the position, the organization and its philosophy, which will help to begin the onboarding process.

Preparing for an Interview

When getting ready for interviews, the following must be kept in mind:

Conducting the Interview

Conducting the interview involves greeting the candidate and developing a good and professional appearance.

The candidate must be asked the questions on the list created prior to the job interview. The candidate's reaction needs to be analyzed with no bias. Moreover, the interviewer should attempt to make the candidate feel comfortable.

It is crucial to actively listen intently to the candidate's replies. Feedback may be provided throughout the job interview or after, based on the interviewer's preference.

Post-interview Evaluations

Post-interview assessments are a vital component of the entire selection procedure. HR personnel perform these assessments to evaluate candidates' performance.

These assessments consist of grading the applicants based on the following:

- Specific questions connected with the job
- Prior expertise in the field
- Integrity and commitment to the task

These scores are then compared with the scores of various other applicants. This selection procedure is also conducted by a panel of directors.

Types of Interviews

In the selection process of completely new personnel, interviews play a crucial role. They help to make certain the ideal candidate for the task is picked.

Business organizations hold two major kinds of interviews to evaluate candidates—structured and unstructured.

Structured Interviews

In a structured interview, the interviewer uses predefined questions to assess candidates. In this particular instance, points or grades are given to every individual based on their answer.

Structured interviews are frequently utilized in extensive recruitment processes in which a lot of candidates are interviewed for one job. They help get rid of prejudices and subjectivity in the interview procedure.

A typical instance would be a behavioral interview, in which the interviewer asks a candidate to give specific examples of prior experiences which align with the job demands.

Unstructured Interviews

In an unstructured interview, the interviewer doesn't stick to predetermined questions. These kinds of interviews are carried out in a more casual, conversational atmosphere.

A structured interview gives the interviewer greater knowledge about a person's character, motivation and communication abilities. It may require open-ended questions, enabling candidates to demonstrate their abilities in a much more natural atmosphere.

This informal interview is most likely carried out in a situation in which a person's social communication and behavior skills will be established.

How to Develop Interviewing Skills

The interview phase may be the first chance for HR specialists to evaluate a candidate's eligibility for the project and potential for development within the business. Therefore, HR experts must be equipped with good interviewing skills to ensure they make the correct hiring decisions.

To develop useful interviewing skills, HR professionals must follow these steps:

Create a Summary of Interview Questions

Some typical interview questions include the following:

- Could you let us know about your earlier work and how it pertains to this particular job?
- What would you consider your strengths and weaknesses?
- Share a challenging situation at your job and how you coped with it.
- Why are you intrigued by this role and our company?

Be Conscious of Nonverbal Communication

HR executives need to be conscious of nonverbal communication cues, like body language and tone of voice, since they can offer useful insights into the individual.

A person's interpersonal skills are of particular importance, regardless of the position the individual is being interviewed for. How the individual holds a conservation and answers tough questions tells the interviewer a lot.

Utilize Active Listening

By actively listening, HR experts may better comprehend the person's answers, as well as determine areas that need additional clarification.

Types of Interview Techniques

Several interviewing methods and abilities can be used to determine a person's suitability for a job. They include the following:

Behavioral Interviewing

Behavioral interviewing concentrates on asking questions regarding the applicant's previous experiences and behavior.

The principle behind this method is that the person's previous actions are the greatest indicator of his or her potential actions inside the business.

The interviewer asks about specific circumstances and experiences and searches for examples of the way the person has previously exhibited particular skills or competencies.

Competency-based Interviews

A competency-based interview evaluates the individual's capabilities, talents and capabilities for the project. The interviewer will ask questions about the applicant's previous experiences. This is significant because it helps clarify how the candidate can complete duties at a particular level of skill.

Case Study Interviews

In a case study interview, the person is provided with a real business situation and prompted to offer solutions. It enables the interviewer to examine the applicant's problem-solving, analytical and decision-making abilities.

The potential candidate is provided with a particular issue to resolve and is asked to describe his or her thinking process in dealing with the situation. This is usually achieved with the aid of charts, PowerPoint presentations, videos and photos.

Group Interviews

In a team interview, many individuals are talked to simultaneously, generally in a team environment. This may evaluate the candidates' interpersonal abilities. The team can be asked to complete a specific task in a given amount of time. This shows the applicant's openness, social skills, teamwork and capability to interact with others.

The interviewer will look at how the applicants work together and search for examples of collaboration and leadership.

Panel Interviews

A panel interview consists of a group of interviewers who may be representatives from several departments in the business, each having certain aspects of expertise.

These kinds of interviews are carried out when the task designation calls for a greater level of intelligence and responsibility.

Unstructured Interviews

An unstructured interview is much more open-ended, enabling the speaker to obtain information much more easily. This type of job interview is helpful for acquiring information about candidates' motives, interests and characteristics.

Interviewing Errors

The job interview process is the most crucial stage in recruiting because it's a chance for HR managers to evaluate a candidate's ability and eligibility for a specific function.

Interviewers may make errors that could result in wrong hiring decisions. Some common interviewing mistakes include:

Relying on First Impressions

First impressions are essential; however, they shouldn't be the foundation for assessing a person because they could be erroneous and affected by looks, clothes and body language.

Therefore, interviewers must avoid making quick judgments based on initial impressions and instead concentrate on the individual's capabilities, credentials and experience, which are crucial for any business.

Not Clarifying What the Job Requires

It's crucial for interviewers to understand the job requirements and convey them to the individual throughout the job interview. The hiring manager will need to determine if the applicants have the needed experience and skills to do the job efficiently.

Candidate-order Pressure

Interviewing several candidates in succession can result in what's commonly known as the candidate-order mistake. This happens when a person interviews and compares each person to the prior candidate. This can lead the interviewer to make a choice based on relative performance as opposed to complete performance.

In order to prevent this, it's essential for interviewers to take frequent pauses and assess each applicant based on individual worth.

Applicants must be evaluated independently depending on their qualifications and abilities. Grading or scoring will help compare the applicants after the interview, though the interviewer must stay away from comparison throughout the process.

Nonverbal Behavior and Impression Management

Nonverbal body language is a significant sign of whether a prospect is anxious or confident.

Impression management describes the actions, unconscious and conscious, that are used to affect others' perceptions of a person.

Attractiveness, Gender and Race

Interviewers shouldn't make selection decisions based on a person's looks, age or gender. The person's background, abilities and aptitude for the position are what determines job suitability.

Applicant Disability

Interviewers should avoid making selection decisions based on a candidate's disability. In accordance with the Americans with Disabilities Act (ADA), companies must provide adjustments for workers with disabilities.

How to Design a Structured Situational Interview

A situational interview is intended to evaluate a person's capability to deal with certain issues encountered while working for the company. It enables an unbiased evaluation of a person's abilities and experience, lessening the possibility for conscious bias and subjectivity.

A few techniques that help create a situational interview are the following:

Determine the Competencies You Should Assess

Begin by figuring out the essential skills you wish to evaluate, including:

- Problem-solving
- Decision-making
- Correspondence skills
- Teamwork
- Working in challenging situations

These skills must be centered on the job necessities as well as the company's atmosphere.

Make a List of Situations

Produce a list of situations pertinent to the job role, which will most likely test the skills that must be evaluated.

For instance, to determine a person's problem-solving abilities, the individual might be asked to explain exactly how he or she would manage a challenging customer situation.

Create Interview Questions

Depending on the circumstances, creating interview questions will let the interviewer assess the applicant's abilities and expertise. Ensuring the questions are open-ended enables the applicant to give a thorough reply.

How to Conduct an Effective Interview

An effective job interview is crucial to the selection process because it lets the interviewer collect information regarding the applicant and evaluate the person's suitability for the job.

Here are some suggestions on how you can carry out a good interview:

Plan Beforehand

Prior to the interview, review the candidate's résumé and job description, as well as job interview objectives.

Ask Open-ended Questions

Open-ended questions are best for obtaining details from the applicant. For instance, rather than asking if the individual possesses practical experience with project management, ask for specifics relating to tasks the person has handled and the outcomes achieved.

Listen Actively

During the interview, listening actively to the candidate's responses is essential. This means paying attention to what is said, making eye contact and avoiding distractions.

Take Notes

Taking notes during the interview can help you recall important information and make more precise hiring decisions. Inform the candidate ahead of time that you will be taking notes.

Ask Follow-up Questions

After the candidate has answered a question, it's a good idea to ask follow-up questions to get more information.

Follow-up questions are when the interviewer asks open-ended questions, as answering leading questions leads to more questions.

Make the Candidate Feel Comfortable

Creating a welcoming and relaxed atmosphere is vital for getting the most out of the interview. The interviewer can do this by greeting the candidate warmly, being friendly and making small talk before starting the interview.

Ways to Retain Employee Records

There are several best practices that companies can use to make sure their personnel files are managed effectively. These practices include:

Business Records Management

Business records management consists of creating a strategy that handles company files, which includes producing, utilizing, storing and disposing of records. The system must be fashioned to satisfy the company's particular requirements.

The Records Life Cycle

The records life cycle describes the phases of a person's work record, from the document's creation to its disposal. These personnel documents are of great importance since they result in special offers and bonuses and are useful for retirement or insurance plans.

Records Classification and Categories

Records classification and categories entail sorting documents depending on their content, structure and purpose.

Keeping Record Confidentiality

Maintaining record confidentiality includes ensuring employee data is kept private and accessed only by authorized personnel.

Businesses must ensure their records management software is protected and that all staff members are aware of the significance of keeping records confidential.

Making Use of Technology to Retain Employee Records

HR information systems (HRIS) and applicant tracking systems (ATS) automate the process of maintaining data, making it simpler for HR departments to keep close track of personnel information, monitor employee performance and store significant documents and records.

HRIS and ATS supply a secure central repository for worker information, lowering the chance of data loss or unauthorized access. Additionally, they help assure compliance with data protection laws and regulations, like General Data Protection Regulation (GDPR).

With the capability to save and retrieve employee documents electronically, HR departments are able to save time and minimize costs related to physical record-keeping procedures.

These methods offer HR departments useful insights into employee performance and turnover rates, enabling them to make educated choices regarding talent selection and retention methods.

Information to Track Using HR Systems

HR techniques help companies manage a number of HR-related steps and functions.

Demographics

Demographics offer data concerning the age, gender, race, ethnicity and other characteristics of employees. Demographics can help organizations evaluate the diversity of their workforce.

Time-to-hire

Time-to-hire measures the time elapsed from when an open position is posted to when an offer is accepted.

A longer time-to-hire can indicate a lengthy or inefficient recruitment process, while a shorter time-to-hire may indicate a streamlined process or a candidate shortage.

Time-to-fill

Time-to-fill measures the time elapsed from when a position becomes available to when it is filled. It can help organizations assess the overall recruitment process, including the effectiveness of sourcing and screening efforts.

It's a self-analysis of the organization and whether the preliminary tests and interviews were conducted efficiently.

Acceptance Rate

The acceptance rate measures the percentage of offers that candidates accept. A low acceptance rate may indicate that the organization is not offering competitive salaries or benefits or that the job is undesirable.

Cost-per-hire

Cost-per-hire measures the total cost of the recruitment process divided by the number of new hires. It can help organizations assess their recruitment efforts' efficiency and identify cost savings areas.

Time-to-productivity

Time-to-productivity measures the amount of time taken from the time workers begin work to whenever they attain improved productivity. It can present useful insights into the onboarding procedure's success and the effect of staff training and development programs.

Successful development and training programs are vital to lowering time-to-productivity.

New-hire Turnover

New-hire turnover is the number of workers that quit the company within a specific time after being hired. Increased new-hire turnover implies a need for better recruitment and onboarding methods, in addition to a necessity for greater employee retention methods.

Section 2 – Learning and Development

Chapter 4: Training and Developing Employees

Training signifies a business's attempts to increase its workers' productivity.

In this section, we will talk about HR's part in development and training and the instruction types utilized to help workers achieve organizational objectives.

HR's Role in Development and Training

HR responsibilities for developing and training employees include:

- Providing employees with an orientation and guiding them about the work goals and expectations.
- Evaluating an individual's work performance and assigning appropriate tasks.
- Helping employees improve the company's overall performance.

The Purpose of Employee Orientation

The orientation of new employees is the foundation of the future success of an organization. It helps employees get acquainted with the company, other employees, the workplace environment, and skill and productivity expectations.

Setting Expectations in an Orientation

During orientation, objectives are made clear to the employees. It is better to clearly state the work expected from the employees as a group because combined effort yields a better outcome.

The Orientation Process

The orientation process is different for each company as it depends on the position an employee is hired for. But it commonly includes an introduction to the organization, its team members and the rules and regulations to be followed.

The code of conduct is discussed, and an office tour is mandatory to maintain a friendly workplace environment. A presentation is arranged for the new members with old employees in attendance.

Developing an Organizational Learning Strategy

An organizational learning strategy is an organization's plan for its employees' learning. It sets out the skills and competencies needed by the company to develop and sustain a successful business.

The following is a breakdown of how to develop an organizational learning strategy:

Identifying Learning Objectives

Learning objectives are outcomes of instructions written in a brief and to-the-point manner.

Usually, learning objectives comprise four components: A, B, C and D – Audience, Behavior, Condition and Degree. They are specific, attainable and time-bound.

Moreover, learning objectives are categorized as follows:

- Cognitive
- Psychomotor
- Affective
- Social

Aligning Organizational Strategy and Training

Training with organizational strategy ensures better results are achieved as it defines the future goals and the areas that are lacking or need improvement. It also promotes specific skills required to further expand the company.

There are different types of strategies that can be used in training, which include the following:

- Competitive
- Corporate
- Business
- Functional
- Operating

Aligning strategy with training ensures the employees understand the expectations necessary to succeed. It also sheds light on the organization's priorities and helps maintain a positive organizational learning culture.

Using the ADDIE Five-Step Training Process

The ADDIE model is a methodology that helps organize and streamline course content. It is a five-step process that develops training systematically and is crucial for designing effective learning and training.

The model consists of the following steps:

Analysis: Comprises analyzing the situation and understanding the gaps or the issues that need to be resolved.

Design: Involves designing the best learning activity to help those involved better understand or respond to the issue. Clear learning objectives and testing strategies should be established.

Development: The step where the design comes together as the final product and learning resources are generated with media support.

Implementation: Before the engagement of the participants, proper preparation is required for a course that an instructor or a facilitator will lead. The group is then notified.

Evaluation: This shows the progress of the previous phases by demonstrating how well the instructional goals were accomplished.

Types of Training

Training is a process of improving job-related skills and acquiring new knowledge for the employees for the betterment of the organization. There are different types of training.

On-the-Job Training

This training is provided at the workplace and is a practical approach to acquiring new skills needed for a real working environment. The most popular example is an internship, which allows individuals to work in a particular role, improving work motivation, employee confidence and productivity.

Apprenticeship Training

Apprenticeship education includes coaches that share how a particular task is done and what they've experienced in the field firsthand.

Chunking

Chunking is a technique in which complex information or learning material is broken down into small pieces or chunks that are easier to consume. It makes learning and retaining information easier. An example of chunking is putting a sentence or a number into two groups.

Informal Training

Informal training is casual training without specific or time-limited goals. Typically, participants don't know what to expect or are unaware they are in training.

Job Instruction Training

In job instruction training, simple instructions are given step by step. It is often used in a practical setup where individuals are experts in manual skills. The trainer is typically an employee at the company.

Programmed Learning

Programmed learning is self-administered knowledge gained at a comfortable pace. The learner consumes the information, comprehends it and is then tested on it, with results immediately given.

Programmed learning requires active participation and is beneficial for learning success. The principles of this method include information given in small steps, active response, self-paced learning and self-evaluation.

The primary advantage of this technique is that everyone can comfortably learn at their own pace without feeling pressure.

Vestibule Training

This is a training method that focuses on employee job education training. It is carried out in a place other than the primary working unit. An example of this is airline pilots who are trained in a simulated cockpit.

Electronic Performance Support System (EPSS)

An electronic performance support system (EPSS) is software designed to train individuals and improve user performance. EPSS is used to provide in-time training with operational experience as it provides the exact information the user needs to solve a problem.

This type of training reduces the cost of training the staff manually while increasing their performance because they can easily use the EPSS to resolve issues at the workplace.

Videoconferencing

Videoconferencing is an online meeting where two or more people can discuss a topic via a video call. It is beneficial when all the participants cannot be physically present in a single location at a certain time.

Computer-based Training (CBT)

With computer-based training, the means of delivery of material or information is a computer. CBT allows the employees and the organization more control over the learning process. The information needed can easily be accessed through a smartphone or a tablet.

Online/Internet-based Training

Through online learning, employees can learn anytime, anywhere. An instructor can lead this training virtually, or employees can learn at their own pace.

This type of training is flexible and affordable and makes time management easier.

Team Training

Training workers as a team will make them work harder, leading to healthy competition and increased productivity.

Learning Curves

Learning curves are graphical representations of the relationship between the proficiency of people performing a task and the amount of experience they have. They help track training progress and predict performance.

These curves are a visual representation of how long it takes to learn a new skill. There are four types of learning curves.

Diminishing Curve: The rate of progress increases rapidly at the beginning but then decreases over time. It signals that trainees have reached their limit or are not determined to learn anymore. The diminishing curve is usually observed where a task is easy to learn, so the learning progression is initially rapid.

Increasing Curve: The rate of progress is slow in the beginning but then gradually increases until full proficiency is achieved. This curve is observed when a task is hard and the initial progress is slow.

Increasing-decreasing Curve: This shows a new learner as the learning is slow in the beginning. Later the learner becomes proficient and takes less time to perform the task. This curve often ends in a plateau.

Complex Learning Curve: The beginning of the curve shows slow learning. Later the curve shows an increase, indicating that the learner is improving at performing the task.

In-house vs. External Training

Internal training is carried out by mentors who work for the same company, while external training, as the name suggests, is carried out by a person not working for the organization.

In-house training requires preparation, such as choosing the topics and the venue and organizing the whole training module. Once it is carried out, other sessions can be carried out using the same training material.

Professionals and experienced instructors lead external training programs, but these are usually general in their approach because they aren't specifically tailored to the company's needs.

How to Create a Training Program

Developing a learning program calls for careful planning.

Determine the Training Objectives: Start by figuring out the exact knowledge or skills that the training program must impart to employees.

Evaluate Employee Needs: Evaluate workers' present knowledge and skills to determine the areas that require improvement. This data may be obtained through assessments, interviews or worker interviews.

Decide Delivery Method: Determine the best technique for providing the instruction, like classroom training, online classes or in-the-field training.

Create the Information: Create the instructional materials, including slides, handouts or web-based modules. This content must be matched with the instructional objectives and staff requirements.

Select a Teacher: Pick a coach who's informed about the topic and has excellent coaching skills. This individual may be an internal worker or an outside advisor.

Plan the Training: Determine the ideal time and place of the training, thinking about employees' schedules and goals.

Assess the Effectiveness: Measure the training course's effect on worker performance and make needed adjustments. This could be accomplished by means of assessments, interviews or performance indices.

Watch Progress: Regularly track the development of workers through the training plan.

How to Assess the Training Effort

Evaluating the training effort is a crucial stage in guaranteeing the efficiency and accomplishment of a training course. The review process helps to determine areas for improvement and figure out if the training plan has fulfilled its objectives.

Here are a few strategies for checking training efforts:

Pre- and Post-training Assessments: These assess the knowledge and abilities the individual has before and after the training course, indicating its efficacy.

Observations: Observing individuals during the training course and at work can offer useful data on the usefulness of the instruction as well as assistance in determining areas for improvement.

Surveys and Feedback: Gathering feedback from participants through surveys or one-on-one meetings can provide valuable insight into their experiences and opinions of the training program.

Performance Evaluations: Measuring employees' performance on the job following the training course can assess the training's effectiveness in helping them do their work tasks better.

Return on Investment (ROI) Analysis: This analysis measures the financial benefits of the training program, including cost savings, increased productivity and improved job performance.

It's important to regularly evaluate training programs to make necessary adjustments and improvements and to ensure that they meet the needs of the participants and the organization.

Ways to Measure Training Effectiveness

There are several ways through which training effectiveness can be measured. This method should be decided before the beginning of the training. Some of these are as follows:

Time Series Design

The time series design statistically analyzes the effects of the training on learners before and after the training.

For example, a manufacturing company measures the workers' productivity every month for a year and training is scheduled every two months. This way, the company measures employees' productivity before and after the training.

Controlled Experimentation

Controlled experimentation is often used in health care, especially when testing drugs. All variables are held constant in controlled experimentation, so uncertainties cannot influence the results.

This study has two groups and the participants are chosen randomly from different demographics, so the division between the control and experimental groups is equivalent.

An excellent example is testing the effects of a drug. The control group is given the placebo, and the experimental group is given the drug, while all other variables, such as age or sex, are kept similar.

The only difference between these two groups is the variable of taking the medication.

Learning Management Systems

Learning management systems (LMS) manage, distribute and track employee training. They can also track training effectiveness and assess the specific learning process or skill.

Common features of LMS include course creation and management, course calendars and online assessments.

Metrics

Metrics detail quantitative measures utilized to assess or evaluate a specific facet or process. In instruction and advancement, measures are employed to evaluate and monitor the quality and effectiveness of training courses.

Typical indicators utilized in assessing training programs are attendance, completion, knowledge retention, job performance enhancement and ROI.

The choice of indicators is dependent upon the goals and objectives of the training course. Measurements help determine the training course's effect on the business and find opportunities for improvement for upcoming training efforts.

Participant Surveys and Questionnaires

Participant surveys and questions are utilized to collect responses from trainees to evaluate the success of a training plan.

These tools will assist companies in deciding whether the coaching course meets the requirements and expectations of the participants, determine areas for development and assess the general effect of the instruction.

They usually consist of inquiries concerning the course's content, delivery and general worth. The feedback gathered using these tools can be utilized to enhance the training program and improve participant satisfaction, as well as improve the general usefulness of the instruction.

Pre- and Post-testing

Pre- and post-testing are evaluation techniques employed to assess the usefulness of a training plan.

Testing performed just before the training course evaluates the individual's present knowledge, abilities and capabilities. The outcomes of pretesting supply a basis against which the end result of the post-testing can be compared.

The post-testing results are then compared with the pretesting results to determine whether the coaching course has successfully attained its objectives. This assessment can help businesses decide if the coaching plan is beneficial and whether the system ought to be continued, modified or stopped.

After-action Review

An after-action review (AAR) is an organized procedure to assess a training course, project or another company venture. It's generally conducted right after the task's end and entails a review of what was done effectively, what might be enhanced and what lessons have been learned.

An AAR is designed to determine areas for development and guarantee that the knowledge acquired from the project is put toward upcoming jobs.

The AAR process usually consists of reviewing documents, talking to participants and getting feedback from stakeholders.

Chapter 5: Organizational Development and Change Programs

While HR's responsibility is to manage the individuals that make up an organization, its ultimate goal is to see the entire organization thrive. Implementing an organizational development (OD) strategy is one way to ensure this.

OD is based on factual information about the company's strengths and weaknesses; these are then critically analyzed to strategize ways to enhance the company's efficiency.

One way to actualize OD is through implementing change programs.

What Are Organizational Development Programs?

OD programs use an outcome of the OD strategy to improve the company's overall performance.

To be effective, OD programs should be designed to have the following characteristics:

Strategic

Successful OD programs should be based on a well-defined strategy. The outcome of such a program should help the organization meet its strategic goals.

Far-sightedness

The focus of an OD program should bring about a positive change that has a long-lasting effect.

Versatility

An organization is an amalgamation of different departments necessary to help achieve its ultimate goal and vision. So, an effective OD program brings about a comprehensive change in how it addresses various problems and identifies their root causes.

Synergetic

OD programs are mindful of the importance of giving due diligence to the people that make up the organization.

They bring about a change that helps participants transition from their current state to a future state that is efficient and continually progressive.

Customized

Every organization has its own unique set of challenges. To successfully overcome them requires an OD program tailored to the organization's concerns.

HR's Role in Organizational Development

- HR can evaluate whether a program was effective by:
- Promoting development and learning among the workforce
- Enhancing management and leadership abilities
- Devising training programs
- Administering talent management programs.
- Developing coaching programs
- Encouraging innovation and creativity

Managerial On-the-Job Rotation and Training

Managerial on-the-job rotation enables supervisors and future managers to improve their abilities by doing work in different departments within the business.

The objective of on-the-job instruction is to provide managers with a wider comprehension of the business and its activities and enable them to build the skills and understanding they need to guide their teams efficiently.

Managerial rotation is a strategy where administrators are moved from one function to another inside the business to supply them with a wide knowledge of various parts of the company.

It is designed to help executives obtain a more complete knowledge of the company and its activities.

Both managerial on-the-job rotation and training plans may be helpful in improving the skills and capabilities of managers.

Advantages of On-the-Job Training

A few of the advantages of on-the-job training are:

Increased Productivity: By offering hands-on education, workers can master the skills and processes required to do their tasks better, resulting in enhanced productivity.

Reduced Training Costs: On-the-job training is oftentimes cheaper as opposed to other types of education, including classroom-style education, as there's no requirement for materials, teachers or travel costs.

Increased Employee Satisfaction: By enabling personnel to acquire new abilities and accept extra responsibilities, on-the-job training can improve employee satisfaction and lessen turnover.

Customized Training: On-the-job training may be customized to each worker's distinct requirements and capabilities.

Immediate Application: On-the-job training enables personnel to apply what they've learned to their job, making the training more pertinent and effective.

Improved Employee Engagement: By supplying workers with possibilities for development and growth, on-the-job training can improve motivation and employee engagement.

Types of On-the-Job Training

Organizations can utilize several types of on-the-job training techniques to improve their personnel's knowledge and skills. The most common types of in-house training include:

Job Rotation

Job rotation is a knowledge and development approach by which workers are moved from a single task to another within the company, typically for a specific time period. It can be especially beneficial for staff members that wish to take leadership positions or who are planning for promotion within the company.

Coaching

Coaching is a technique that involves a one-on-one connection between a coach and a coachee. The coach gives assistance, direction, feedback and guidance to assist coachees in enhancing their performance and attaining their objectives.

The teaching approach may be utilized in a number of aspects of life, like individual development, leadership development and career advancement, among others.

Understudy Approach

The understudy strategy is an in-office training in which a worker is matched with a competent partner to understand the skills necessary for a particular function.

It's frequently used in the financial, technology and health care sectors, where it's essential to have a strong knowledge of systems and processes. This method can be advantageous since it enables workers to learn through hands-on experience and observation and get assistance and advice from their coach.

The understudy method may also help ensure that vital skills and knowledge are transferred inside a company because the understudies become acquainted with the job and can step in if more seasoned colleagues leave the business or move to an alternative place in the company.

Action Learning

Action learning is hands-on training that entails workers solving real-world challenges by means of a collaborative approach. It focuses on learning by carrying out tasks and allows personnel to put into action the principles they've discovered.

Participants work in small groups to detect issues, collect information and create solutions. Workers develop critical thinking and problem-solving abilities and acquire experience in various facets of the company.

Action learning is generally utilized to acquire management and leadership abilities and help cross-functional collaboration and continual improvement projects.

Stretch Assignments

A stretch assignment is a task provided to workers that's outside of their standard job duties or which calls for abilities they haven't yet established.

The goal of a short-term assignment is to challenge people and enable them to improve and enhance their abilities. Stretch tasks are generally provided to high-potential workers as a means of readying them for later leadership roles,

The advantages of stretch tasks include greater job satisfaction, improved motivation and better work performance. In addition, stretch projects can present workers with new perspectives, enhance their knowledge of various facets of the company and improve their professional community.

Off-the-Job Management Training and Development Techniques

Off-the-job management and development are strategies for instruction and advancement which happen outside the regular work environment. This can result in better work performance, greater work satisfaction and career development possibilities.

On-the-job knowledge and development seek to offer supervisors the expertise, skills and capabilities needed to do their jobs efficiently.

Some typical subjects in on-the-job management knowledge and development may include leadership, project management, team building, communication and financial control.

On-the-job management instruction and development could consist of several techniques, including:

The Case Study Method

The case study method is a teaching and learning approach that calls for the evaluation of real-life circumstances usually employed in business and leadership training. It provides a scenario and challenges learners to determine the major problems, collect and analyze information and make suggestions and answers.

This method simulates real-life circumstances, enabling pupils to apply their skills and knowledge to practical issues and cultivate problem-solving skills and critical thinking.

Furthermore, the case study technique is frequently used together with tutorials along with other educational materials and could entail group discussions, presentations and individual or group projects.

Management Games

Management games, such as Interpret, are development techniques that simulate real-life business scenarios in a controlled and safe environment.

These games allow participants to practice their decision-making and problem-solving skills and gain a deeper understanding of how organizations work.

In management games, participants are divided into teams and assigned roles within a simulated company. The teams then compete against each other to achieve set goals and objectives.

The games often involve financial, marketing and production challenges, and the decisions made by the teams will impact their results.

By taking part in management games, people can improve their leadership and interpersonal skills, learn about various company capabilities and the way they communicate with one another while obtaining insights into how they can make good decisions under stress.

Outside Seminars

Outside seminars are professional development events that occur beyond a business.

Industry professionals ordinarily lead these workshops and offer attendees the newest information and strategies in a particular region. They may address a variety of subjects, such as management, leadership, finances, marketing and HR.

Outside seminars may be online or in person, ranging from half-day workshops to multi-day seminars. They're a favorite type of on-the-job knowledge and advancement because they offer an organized and focused learning environment and a pause from the daily work schedule.

University-related Programs

University-related programs include management knowledge and development programs. These applications can be in the form of degree programs, like a master's degree in business administration (MBA), or non-degree programs, like short classes or workshops.

University-related programs enable executives to improve their skills and knowledge, connect with other individuals and obtain an extensive perspective on diverse business problems and trends.

The program for these packages can be quite extensive, dealing with topics including leadership, strategy, finance, marketing and organizational behavior, among other things.

Role-playing

Role-playing is a teaching and development method where participants assume the roles of people in a real situation and act out a circumstance or issue. In a role-playing exercise, students can practice communication skills, decision-making and problem-solving, along with various other behaviors appropriate to the simulation.

Role-playing is frequently used in management knowledge and development to assist participants in figuring out how they can deal with tough situations that might develop in the office.

Executive Coaches

Executive coaches are specialized mentors working with professionals, senior managers and other leaders to assist them in attaining their professional objectives and enhancing their leadership abilities.

Executive coaching might entail helping individuals one-on-one, in teams and inside an organizational setting.

Managing Organizational Change Programs

Organizational change programs are created to assist a company in moving from its present condition to its desired future state. These programs can include a number of modifications, such as changes to processes, systems, culture, structure and technologies.

Managing organizational change plans may be complicated since it requires working with numerous parties, including staff members, managers, clients, suppliers and shareholders.

Below are several crucial steps in establishing organizational change programs:

Determine the Change: Clearly spell out the change program's aim, scope and objectives.

Communicate the Change: Share the alteration with all the participants and point out why the modification is needed. Promote open and transparent communication regarding the change.

Engage Stakeholders: Get involved with important stakeholders in the transformation process to ensure they feel committed to the change. It may include staff, supervisors, clients, suppliers and shareholders.

Evaluate the Impact: Evaluate the effect of the modification on all players and figure out the materials and support required to effectively execute the change.

Create a Strategy: Develop a plan for executing the change, which includes a time frame, budget and roles and duties.

Implement the Change: Execute the program, keep track of progress and deal with any difficulties that occur.

Assess the Change: Assess the transformation system's outcomes and determine if the desired results have been attained. If not, make essential alterations.

Reinforce the Change: Reinforce the modification by integrating it into the company's culture and procedures. Celebrate accomplishments and continue to make clear the advantages of the transformation.

Objectives of Organizational Change

The aim of organizational change is to boost the company's general performance, competitiveness and efficiency. It may differ based on the company's present objectives and challenges, though a few typical factors for organizational change consist of the following:

- Adjusting to the altering business landscape and market conditions
- Increasing operational effectiveness and productivity
- Improving innovation and inventive problem-solving
- Developing and maintaining top talent
- Improving the organization's standing and brand image
- Responding to new laws or compliance requirements

Organizational change initiatives may take several forms, such as restructuring, process improvement, technology application, cultural change initiatives and leadership training courses.

No matter the particular modification plan, the main objective is to help the business reach its desired effects and stay competitive in a rapidly developing business environment.

What is Change Management?

Change management refers to the action of determining, planning and carrying out organizational modifications in a structured and controlled fashion.

The aim of change control is usually to lessen the effect of change on staff, partners and the company overall while making sure that the advantages of change are fulfilled.

Change management entails a number of tasks, such as evaluating the demand for change, presenting the shift to stakeholders, carrying out the change and keeping tabs on the outcomes of the shift.

Good change management calls for effective leadership, clear communication, cooperation and a focus on addressing the requirements of all parties involved. It must also be managed, which can be achieved using the subsequent change management systems.

Lewin's Change Management Model

Lewin's Change Management Model is a well-known framework for controlling organizational change. The system was created by Kurt Lewin, a psychotherapist and change management specialist, and has three phases: unfreeze, transition and refreeze.

Unfreeze: The first stage of Lewin's Change Management Model is the unfreezing stage, where the current status quo is questioned and the need for change is identified. During this stage, individuals may resist change due to their attachment to the current way of doing things.

Transition: The second stage of the model is the change stage, where new ideas and behaviors are introduced and implemented. This stage is focused on breaking down old habits and building new ones.

Refreeze: The final stage of the model is the refreeze stage, where the new changes are consolidated and stabilized to become the new norm. This stage focuses on embedding the changes into the organizational culture and ensuring they are sustainable over the long term.

Kotter's 8-Step Model for Change

Kotter's 8-Step Model for Change is a framework developed by John Kotter, a renowned Harvard Business School professor and change management expert.

The model provides a systematic approach to managing change in organizations and outlines the following eight steps:

1 – Establish a Sense of Urgency: Create a sense of urgency around the need for change.

2 – Form a Strong Coalition: Gather a coalition of individuals with all the abilities necessary to guide change.

3 – Develop a Vision for Change: Create a perspective to guide the modification effort and help people realize what the change could be like.

4 – Explain the Vision: Communicate the vision in a fashion that motivates individuals to help work for improvement.

5 – Empower Others to Act on the Vision: Provide individuals with all the equipment and information they need to act.

6 – Create Short-Term Wins: Identify and attain some immediate wins which help develop momentum and demonstrate that change is achievable.

7 – Consolidate Gains and Produce More Change: Use the vigor from short-term wins to push a lot more shifts and attain more important results.

8 – Anchor New Approaches in the Organization's Culture: Institutionalize the changes, making them a permanent part of the organization's culture.

By following these steps, organizations can increase the chances of successful change and minimize resistance.

ADKAR Change Management Model

ADKAR is a change management model produced by Prosci, a research and instruction business specializing in change management.

The acronym ADKAR stands for awareness, ability, knowledge, desire and reinforcement. The model offers a framework for understanding the primary components of effective change and the way they communicate with one another.

Based on the ADKAR model, change management has five steps:

1. Raising awareness of the demand for change among stakeholders.
2. Building a desire to have change, including gaining buy-in and commitment from stakeholders.
3. Increasing understanding and knowledge of the change, which includes the procedures and skills necessary to implement the change.
4. Emphasizing the improvement of the needed resources and skills required to create the change.
5. Stressing the value of reinforcement, including efforts that are ongoing to maintain the change as time passes.

Kübler-Ross Change Curve

The Kübler-Ross model was originally developed to describe the grief process that individuals go through when facing death and dying, but it has since been applied to various change management scenarios, including organizational change, personal change and more.

It assists people and groups in realizing that change is a procedure and that it's common to undergo a variety of feelings throughout the process.

The Kübler-Ross Change Curve outlines the five stages of grief that individuals go through when faced with change. The five stages are:

- **Denial:** This phase requires denying that change is happening or necessary.
- **Anger:** This phase is characterized by emotions of frustration, anger, and resentment toward the change.
- **Bargaining:** This stage entails attempting to negotiate ways to mitigate the effect of the change.

- **Depression:** This phase involves being sad, hopeless and bogged down by the change.
- **Acceptance:** This stage requires accepting the shift and moving forward.

Bridges Transition Model

The Bridges Transition Model is a framework that identifies the mental stages that men and women undergo whenever they encounter organizational change. The model was created by William Bridges, an American organizational consultant and writer.

The model consists of three phases:

Endings: This is the first stage, in which individuals are faced with a feeling of grief and loss about the changes happening within the organization. It's a period for them to process the conclusion of the present condition and admit that everything is changing.

The Neutral Zone: This is the point where people are in a state of uncertainty and ambiguity about the future. They might feel confusion, frustration and strain.

New Beginnings: This is the last stage, in which people start to find out the change's potential advantages and embrace it. They develop a feeling of clarity, direction and hope for the long term.

The Bridges Transition Model is often used in change management to allow businesses to understand and control the mental effect of change. Businesses can better support people and develop a more optimistic change experience by recognizing the stages and emotions related to change.

Section 3 – Compensation and Benefits

Chapter 6: Compensation: Establishing Strategic Pay Plans

Employee compensation is a critical component of every business since it displays the worth of a worker's wages along with incentives. Compensation has different types, such as immediate cash compensation, benefits and indirect compensation.

An effective compensation program can help businesses keep a competitive edge in the labor market and improve their profits. Based on the market, the dimensions of the organization and the location, pay packages can be quite different.

Business sectors such as technology and finance tend to be recognized for paying great salaries and providing numerous advantages.

What's Included in Employee Compensation?

Employee compensation is any money or benefits paid to employees in exchange for their labor.

Organizations can compensate their employees in two primary forms:

Direct Compensation

Direct compensation consists of an employee's monetary reward for executing work. It is often the most visible and transparent component of an employee's compensation and includes:

Base Salary: This is the minimum amount you anticipate earning for your time or services before adding benefits, bonuses or compensation. Base pay is hourly, weekly, monthly or annually.

Wages: These are the monetary remuneration paid to employees in exchange for their labor and services. Wages are usually paid hourly for temporary or contract-based jobs and are typically determined by criteria like an employee's experience, education, abilities and the type of work individuals undertake.

Commissions: These are given when employees sell a product or service and receive a portion of the overall sale value as their pay.

Bonuses: These are usually provided as a reward for meeting or exceeding performance targets and as an incentive to encourage personnel to attain particular business goals.

Indirect Compensation

Besides the starting salary, a worker might get nonmonetary bonuses or awards from a company, known as indirect compensation. These may take different forms, such as:

Health Insurance: Employers usually provide health insurance as a benefit. This allows employees to get medical treatment without paying the entire price out of pocket.

Retirement Plans: Organizations typically provide retirement plans to entice and retain talent. These plans allow workers to save for retirement with employer contributions.

Vacations: Vacations offered by the employer are a typical employee benefit. Vacations give employees much-needed relaxation, enhancing their overall job performance and reducing burnout.

How Are Employees Paid?

Employers commonly pay employees by direct deposit, paper check or electronic payment platform. The quantity and frequency of payment can vary based on employee position, industry and employer requirements.

There are two methods of employee payments:

Increments of Time: Depending on the employer's rules and the type of work the employee does, there are different ways to pay in terms of time increments. Hourly, weekly, biweekly, semi-monthly and monthly pay schedules are the most common.

Payments on Performance: Employees may receive additional compensation based on their performance and base pay, which can take the shape of bonuses, commissions, profit-sharing or stock options, among others.

Basic Factors in Determining Pay Rates

There are several factors you should consider before establishing a pay rate. These include:

Aligning Total Rewards with Strategy

Aligning total rewards with strategy involves designing and implementing compensation and benefits plans that meet the strategic goals and objectives of the firm. It is a combination of an employer's benefits, perks, incentives, guidelines, processes and other forms of rewards.

Equity and Its Effect on Pay Rates

This is based on the equity principle of motivation; people desire equity and fairness. Individuals use this idea to judge whether they are being treated fairly by comparing their input-to-reward ratio to the ratios of others in comparable positions.

When determining compensation rates, employers should consider the following types of equity:

External Equity: This refers to the fairness and equity of pay and rewards for a particular profession or skill level relative to similar jobs or skill levels in the external labor market. It is founded on the premise that a company's pay rates should be comparable with those of other businesses in the same industry and region.

Internal Equity: This refers to an organization's fairness and equality of pay and rewards. Internal equity is founded on the concept that employees who perform comparable jobs or have similar abilities and experience should receive equal pay.

Individual Equity: This refers to the fairness of a person's pay relative to what coworkers get for similar work in the organization, based on each person's performance.

Procedural Equity: This is the perception of the fairness of the procedures and processes used to decide the allocation of rewards. Individuals assess the fairness and transparency of the methods used to determine incentives and their participation in the decision-making process.

Legal Considerations in Compensation

Depending on the particular rules and regulations of the jurisdiction where the employee is being compensated, the legal concerns involved in payment may differ.

Common legal considerations may include maintaining compliance with minimum wage laws, tax laws and other labor laws, such as:

The Davis-Bacon Act: A federal law that says contractors and subcontractors who work on federally funded construction projects must compensate their employees no less than the local pay rates and perks for a comparable job.

Walsh-Healey Public Contracts Act: A federal law that pertains to contracts for producing or providing items, supplies or resources for government-operated or government-owned institutions. It helps make sure that federal agencies pay their workers. The law also guarantees contractors pay their workers more than the current minimum wage and adhere to other labor laws.

Title VII of the Civil Rights Act: Federal legislation prohibiting unfair hiring and firing methods, pay discrimination and harassment. The law prohibits employment discrimination based on race, sex, faith, color and ethnic origin. The statute additionally pertains to businesses with a minimum of fifteen personnel, labor unions and employment agencies.

The Fair Labor Standards Act: A labor law stating the proper minimum salary and overtime pay at "time and a half" for hours worked greater than forty each week.

Work-Related Law (FLSA Clauses): A federal law setting minimum requirements for workers' working hours, earnings, premium overtime compensation and employment records.

Union Influences on Compensation Decisions and Pay Policies

Unions can significantly influence a business's salary choices and pay rules and regulations. By way of collective bargaining, unions work with companies to create minimum wage rates and pay scales, along with any other compensation-related policies and practices.

Additionally, associations might pay equity and fairness, affecting the pay distribution across work roles and levels. They might even use industrial action and strikes to convince corporations to meet their wage demands.

In trade unionized workplaces, trade unions can be important in creating remuneration procedures.

The National Labor Relations Act (NLRB), which the National Labor Relations Board (NLRB) implements, links trade labor organizations. It manages workers' rights to participate in collective bargaining, establish and become members of a union and creates procedures for union elections and issues regarding unfair labor practices.

Pay Policies

Pay policies are the rules and guidelines organizations work with to determine just how much they pay their personnel for their work. A few of these procedures involve establishing salaries, choosing increases and bonuses and creating benefits packages.

These procedures ensure personnel are compensated equally and fairly for their job and assist businesses in attracting and maintaining the best employees in a competitive environment.

Paying Expatriate Employees

Paying expatriate workers implies providing them with a wage and other rewards when they work in a different nation, whether for a short period or a long time. Due to expenses such as living, housing, education and getting accustomed to a new society, expatriates generally get paid a lot more than hometown workers.

Organizations pay expatriates using the following approaches:

The Balance Sheet Approach: This is a common way of compensating expatriate employees. This approach seeks to ensure expatriates are not financially worse off than if they were working in their native country.

The Localization Approach: This is a method for rewarding expatriate personnel based on the typical compensation levels in the host country, as opposed to the employees' salary in their home country. The approach seeks to treat expats as local employees and can simplify the compensation procedure, but it may lead to wage inequities.

Independent Contractor Compensation

Independent contractor remuneration is a payment arrangement between an organization and an independent contractor who performs specific services or project-based work.

Individual contractors' payment is frequently decided in advance and can be hourly, weekly, daily or a flat rate for the whole task. They're accountable for taxes, insurance and other work-related expenses; therefore, their salary is generally above that of in-office personnel.

Generally, the payment terms are outlined in the proper agreement, which might contain provisions for bonuses, bonuses and penalties for inadequate work.

There are several requirements to consider before creating an independent contractor's compensation. These include:

The Equal Pay Act: The EPA requires that companies pay women and men equally for carrying out tasks that call for similar capability, effort and duty under identical working conditions.

The Employee Retirement Income Security Act: ERISA sets up minimum requirements for employee benefit programs, like health and retirement programs. It requires employers to supply plan members with important information, including the plan's management and funding, eligibility requirements and plan participants' duties and rights.

The Age Discrimination in Employment Act: ADEA forbids employment discrimination against people aged 40 and older in hiring, firing, promotion, salary and other terms and conditions of employment.

The Americans with Disabilities Act: The ADA forbids discrimination against people with disabilities. It requires all employers to give reasonable accommodations to individuals with disabilities so that they can perform essential tasks.

How to Set Pay Rates

Employers determine employee pay rates depending on various factors, including job analysis and description, skills and experience, supply and demand, performance, company financials and legal requirements.

Two main methods are used to determine a pay rate. They are:

The Job Evaluation Method: A method for figuring out how important or valuable different jobs are in an organization. This approach means comparing the requirements, responsibilities and skills needed for each job to figure out how important each one is and set up a fair pay system.

A Market-Based Approach: This strategy entails exploring and analyzing the pay amounts of comparable jobs in the labor market. It seeks to ensure a company's pay rates complement the market prices to please and keep employees.

How to Perform a Job Evaluation

Let us take a look at the way to carry out a job evaluation.

Identify the Demand: Work assessment helps a business determine the need for a specific role by looking at the job's value inside the firm's hierarchy. This assessment can help in determining gaps in the company's structure, which can require developing new jobs and making certain sources are allocated effectively and efficiently.

Get Employees to Cooperate: This is when workers are needed to provide thorough information regarding their work tasks, experience and skills.

Choose Work Evaluation Committee: Organizations can select a task evaluation committee that is well equipped to make choices about employment evaluations and pay rates. This will help make sure that the procedure of assessing a task is accurate and fair in line with the objectives of the business.

Ranking Method for Job Evaluation

The task ranking technique orders tasks based on how critical they are toward the company. The duties and demands of the job owner decide the importance of the job order.

The ranking of jobs involves:

Obtaining Job Information: Create rankings based on the prepared job descriptions for each position.

Selecting and Grouping Jobs: You can rank jobs simultaneously; however, most of the time, appointments are organized by department or "clusters," such as factory workers and office workers, so you do not have to compare factory and office jobs directly.

Selecting Compensable Factors: In the ranking method, it is common to use one aspect, like job difficulty, to rank jobs based on "the whole job." No matter how many factors you choose, you should carefully explain what each one means to the evaluators so that they can evaluate the jobs similarly.

Ranking Jobs: The easiest way to rank jobs is to give each rater a set of index cards with short descriptions of positions on each one. These cards can then be ranked from worst to best.

Combining Ratings: Put all the jobs ranked into groups or classifications based on what they have in common, such as similar tasks, skills or knowledge needed. All positions in a specific group or type are paid the same amount or within the same range. When this is done, the rating committee can take the average of all the rankings.

Comparing Current Pay Utilizing a Salary Survey: Utilizing a salary survey will help you to determine what the typical pay, together with benefits, is for comparable jobs, industries and places. It provides a holistic picture of how compensation is handled, such as base pay and incentives, together with some other transaction types.

Creating a Revolutionary Pay Scale: A completely new pay scale entails creating a compensation system that includes a method for establishing pay rates within a company. The goal is to ensure workers are compensated fairly according to their work tasks, duties and credentials so that the organization is competitive with different employers within the same sector.

How to Develop a Competitive Pay Plan

Developing a competitive pay program demands a smart and strategic approach that considers market conditions, organizational goals and individual needs.

It involves:

Choosing Benchmark Jobs: Select representative positions that reflect the market in terms of skill level, complexity and pay to create consistency in compensation plans.

Selecting Compensable Factors: Determine the features of employment that define the relative worth of each job within an organization, ensuring fair and competitive compensation based on key factors.

Assigning Weights to Compensable Factors: Emphasize the factors most essential to business objectives by assigning weights to compensable criteria.

Converting Percentages to Points for Each Factor: Establish a clear and consistent point system for evaluating jobs based on the relative value of each compensable factor.

Defining Each Factor's Degrees: Describe the different levels of each factor to evaluate the presence and extent of each compensable factor in a job, crucial for determining the job's relative worth and compensation level.

Evaluating the Jobs: Assess each job's compensable factor level using the defined skill, effort, responsibility, conditions, degrees and allocated points to determine the total number of points for each benchmark job.

Conducting a Market Analysis: Perform an informal salary survey to price jobs and benefits and compare the current wage rates with those of other companies.

Developing Pay Grades and Establishing Rate Ranges: Organize related tasks into grades for compensation purposes and establish vertical pay ranges for each horizontal pay grade.

Addressing Remaining Jobs and Correct Out-of-Line Rates: Add remaining roles and adjust wage rates far from the wage line or outside the rate range.

Developing Compensation Plans for Managers and Professionals

Managers and professionals are usually paid more than other workers because they have specialized knowledge, skills and expertise and play essential organizational roles. They make hard decisions, lead teams and ensure the organization meets its goals. They usually have more education and experience than other employees, which makes them more valuable to the company and justifies paying them more.

That's why developing compensation plans for managers and professionals requires a thorough understanding of their roles, responsibilities and the market value of their skills and experience.

Elements of Professional and Executive Compensation

Professional and executive employee pay usually consists of a mix of components that are meant to engage, retain and inspire employees, such as:

Base Salary: The basic salary is the set amount of payment that workers get in return for their job. It's typically determined by the worker's job duties, abilities and expertise.

Bonuses: Bonuses are a kind of fixed salary generally given to workers according to their effectiveness, the functionality of the organization or both. They can be continuing or one-time and are linked to individual, team or company-wide objectives.

Equity: Equity-based compensation is related to ownership of the firm. This may consist of stock options, restricted stock or other types of equity-based awards.

Benefits: Benefits are non-salary compensation components that might include health insurance, retirement programs and paid time off, along with additional incentives, including gym memberships, driving allowances or college reimbursement.

Perquisites: Perquisites or "perks" are noncash compensation components that provide extra value to workers. These might include corporate automobiles, executive days off and additional advantages.

Career Development Opportunities: Career development opportunities could consist of training courses, mentoring or several other kinds of assistance which help personnel develop their skills.

Chapter 7: Pay for Performance and Benefits

Pay for performance ties employees' pay to how well they perform their jobs and what they bring to the company.

Under this method, employees may get bonuses, commissions or other forms of incentive pay based on how well they meet individual or team goals, how well they do on performance reviews or how well they do on other ways to measure success.

Pay for performance can encourage workers to do better by aligning their goals with the organization's, which helps the business do well. Benefits, on the other hand, are a nonmonetary form of compensation that can include health insurance, plans for saving for retirement, paid time off and other incentives.

Employers can create a supportive and motivating work environment by providing appropriate pay for performance and benefits.

Components of Wage Statements and Payroll Processing

The following components comprise wage statements and payroll processing:

1 – Information About the Employee: This includes the employee's name, address, Social Security Number (SSN) or other tax ID number and additional relevant personal information.

2 – Deductions: These are the amounts taken from an employee's pay for health insurance premiums, retirement contributions or wage garnishments.

3 – Taxation: This includes federal, state and local income taxes, as well as Medicare and Social Security taxes. Taxes are taken from workers' gross pay and sent to the appropriate government agencies on their behalf.

4 – Garnishments: These are court-ordered deductions from an employee's paycheck to pay a debt or legal obligation, like child support, back taxes or a judgment against the employee.

5 – Net Pay: This is the employee's total pay after taxes and other deductions.

What is Incentive Pay?

Incentive pay, commonly referred to as variable pay, is a type of compensation that pays employees for meeting or surpassing performance targets or objectives. Bonuses, commissions, profit-sharing and stock options are a few of the various forms of incentive pay.

By attaching compensation to specific performance objectives, incentive pay aims to encourage people to work harder and more efficiently, which can enhance individual and team performance, boost productivity and drive overall business outcomes.

Incentive pay is commonly employed in industries such as sales, where performance can be easily assessed and rewarded. However, it can also be used in other fields to motivate and compensate people for reaching specified goals or results.

Individual Employee Incentive and Recognition Programs

Individual employee recognition and incentive programs are meant to motivate and recognize individuals for their performance and accomplishments.

Incentives are the prizes and perks utilized to drive positive employee behavior. They include tuition reimbursement, more extended vacations and greater flexibility in work arrangements.

In contrast, employee recognition programs aim to acknowledge the accomplishments of qualified people or teams within an organization. Examples include gift cards, work outings and anniversary celebrations. They enhance employee morale, retain talent and create a connection between employees and the company.

Some other examples of incentive and recognition programs may include:

Piecework

Piecework is a worker reward and recognition system in which employees are compensated based on the number of goods they produce or tasks they finish. It can be utilized in a variety of industries, like manufacturing, construction and farming, in which efficiency and paper can be readily quantifiable.

This system can motivate personnel to perform better and boost their output, leading to increased production and earnings for the company.

Merit Pay as an Incentive

The aim of merit pay would be to encourage individuals to work more effectively by honoring and rewarding their accomplishments to the business.

A great merit pay plan can improve performance, morale and employee engagement, leading to better company results.

Recognition-Based and Non-Financial Awards

Nonmonetary and recognition-based awards are a type of employee motivation and recognition system that honors workers for their achievements along with contributions without providing monetary compensation.

These awards can include certificates, trophies, plaques or public recognition at meeting times and on the company's social networking sites. They're meant to encourage employees and create a healthy work environment where workers feel valued and respected.

Rewards for Salespeople

Commissions on product sales, incentives for achieving sales objectives and bonuses for best performers tend to be typical ways to encourage salespeople.

These incentives may come in various types, such as money, gift cards, trips or several other incentives. They help build a competitive and enjoyable atmosphere, which motivates sales agents to work harder, be more inventive and achieve their objectives.

Sales agents might also be compensated through a range of wage packages based on their employer and the dynamics of their business, such as:

Salary Plan: A starting salary offers a constant income, regardless of sales performance.

Commission Plan: There's a greater likelihood of earning additional cash with commission-only programs but also a better possibility of losing money since the percentage is determined by how many product sales the salesperson generates.

Combination Plan: Because it provides both a starting salary along with a percentage, a combination program provides balance and the opportunity to make more cash. Employees receive a basic salary regardless of product sales. If they meet their sales goals, they also obtain a commission.

Rewards for Managers and Executives

Incentives for managers and executives are awards meant to motivate these people to attain specific goals and objectives. These bonuses are usually influenced by the business's overall performance and can include incentives, profit sharing and stock options, along with other financial awards.

Nonmonetary awards, including lengthy vacation time, flexible employment arrangements and possibilities for professional advancement, may serve as rewards. Let's look at two types of programs.

Total and Long-Term Rewards Packages

Typically, the overall and long-term pay package for managers, along with executives, consists of both nonfinancial and financial incentives. Financial incentives may include basic salary, performance-based incentives, and stock options, along with any other equity-based bonuses.

In comparison, nonmonetary incentives include flexible work schedules, professional development, advancement opportunities and improved benefits like health insurance and pension programs.

Short-term Incentives and the Annual Bonus

Short-term incentives and yearly bonuses are intended to compensate executives and managers for their effectiveness over a particular time, generally a year.

These bonuses are usually associated with certain objectives, such as growing product sales, earning more cash or making sure operations run smoothly. They may contain cash bonuses or equity-based prizes.

Furthermore, annual bonuses may consist of financial and nonfinancial incentives, including earnings sharing, stock options and other advantages.

Team and Organization-wide Incentive Plans

Team and organization-wide incentive programs are created to motivate groups of workers to work in concert toward the same objective or objective. These programs do not need to be monetary.

They intend to get employees to come together, boost performance and ensure workers' interests coincide with the company's objectives.

How to Design Team Incentives

Identify the Team Goals: Determine which business goals the team incentive plan will support and how you will monitor progress.

Determine the Incentive Type: Choose a team-motivating incentive like cash, stock or nonfinancial benefits.

Establish Team Performance Measures: Pick performance metrics to track progress toward incentive targets and set up a system for monitoring and reporting team performance.

Determine the Payout Structure: Establish clear rules and procedures for team eligibility and awards, then calculate and distribute incentive payouts.

Inform Everyone: Share the team incentive plan's goals, key performance indicators (KPIs), payout structure and eligibility restrictions with everyone.

Monitor and Adapt the Strategy: Monitor team performance and adjust the incentive plan as needed to keep it inspiring and rewarding team goals.

Types of Incentive Plans

An incentive plan is a means for a business to reward its workers for attaining a certain goal. Here are some common types of incentive plans:

Profit-Sharing Plans

Profit-sharing plans give employees a direct financial stake in the company's success and can help align their interests with the organization.

Employees get a share of the company's profits based on a formula, such as a certain percentage of the company's annual revenue or net income.

Scanlon Plans

In a Scanlon plan, a team consists of individuals from various departments or positions within the company. The staff is at the forefront of discovering ways for the business to save cash. The crew might obtain a bonus or some other incentive depending on how much cash they saved.

Gainsharing Plans

Gainsharing programs can be created for a single individual, group or company. Prizes are determined by how much cash the business generates and are generally split between the personnel that helped generate profits.

At-Risk Pay Plans

These are incentive programs that make up a portion of individuals' pay and are determined by how efficiently they perform their work. Employees' salary is "at risk" since it is determined by if they attain or beat their performance objectives.

What are Benefits?

Benefits are non-wage payments that an employer provides. They're intended to give workers additional worth along with their base or hourly salary.

There are numerous kinds of advantages to benefits, such as:

Unemployment Insurance: This is a personal assistance system that will help people who have lost their job or perhaps have been laid off due to no fault of their own to obtain brief financial assistance. Business owners generally purchase the system through state and federal taxes, and local governments administer it.

Holidays and Vacations: Employees are able to take time from work to recuperate. How much vacation time an employer provides can hinge on the company's regulations and how long the worker has been employed.

Sick Leave: This provides workers paid time off to recuperate from a short-term illness, injury or health problem without giving up their earnings.

Severance Pay: This is compensation for a worker that has been terminated. Severance pay is intended to assist as the worker is searching for a new job. The quantity and duration of severance pay might differ from employer to employer and may rely upon the time worked and the work level.

Supplemental Unemployment Benefits: This is additional cash that an employer provides to employees that lose their jobs due to a short-term layoff or a business shutdown.

What Are Insurance Benefits?

Insurance benefits assist personnel in covering insurance costs relating to medical expenses, doctor visits, hospital stays, prescription medications, along with other health expenses.

Oftentimes, the employer pays for all or a portion of these services, though workers might need to spend a percentage of the price of coverage.

These advantages could include:

Workers' Compensation

Workers' compensation provides medical and wage replacement benefits to workers hurt at the office.

This required insurance is meant to guard both personnel and employers in the situation of a work-related illness or injury. It typically covers medical expenses, lost earnings, rehabilitation expenses, as well as disability payments.

Hospitalization, Health and Disability Insurance

In the event of injury or illness, disability insurance, health or hospitalization are provided to help workers with medical treatment and retirement. These advantages might include protection from prescription drugs and preventive care along with medical, medical and hospitalization fees.

In comparison, disability insurance offers income replacement for workers that are permanently or temporarily disabled and not able to perform.

Long-term Care Insurance

Long-term care insurance covers taking care of individuals that can't do things by themselves, such as bathing, dressing and consuming food. It may help cover care in a nursing home, an assisted living facility or the individual's own home.

Life Insurance

Life insurance shields a worker's household financially in the event of funeral expenses, remaining debts, etc.

Benefits for Part-Time and Contingent Workers

Part-time and contingent employees might not be eligible for certain advantages, including retirement plans or health insurance. These advantages can include paid leave, a flexible work schedule, as well as the use of staff assistance programs.

Retirement Benefits

Retirement benefits offer economic protection to personnel when they quit their job. These advantages consist of pensions, 401(k) plans and IRAs, along with additional savings blueprints, which are funded by the employer, the employee or both.

Pension benefits are an essential facet of benefit packages and play an important part in attracting and keeping skilled workers. There are several pension benefits, such as:

Defined Benefit Plans: These are conventional retirement programs wherein a business guarantees to pay workers a particular monthly benefit at retirement that is driven by a system that takes into consideration the employee's years of service and age, along with salary.

Defined Contribution Plans: In these programs, employers and workers make contributions to a retirement account, so the employee's retirement depends on the money contained within the bank account at retirement. Examples of defined contribution plans include 403(b) plans, 401(k) plans, plus individual retirement accounts (IRAs).

Cash Balance Plans: These hybrid designs blend features of defined contribution plans. In a cash balance program, the employer puts aside a portion of a worker's salary yearly. Once retired, the worker is able to get a lump sum payment or an annuity.

Employee Stock Ownership Plans (ESOPs): These plans permit workers to own personal stock in the business they work for, which may offer a pension advantage if the company's stock does very well.

Social Security: This is a federal system that provides retirement, survivor and disability benefits to qualified people and their families. The quantity of Social Security benefits individuals get is determined by their income history and the age at which they begin receiving benefits.

Personal Services and Family-friendly Benefits

Employers offer personal services to help personnel, including childcare, eldercare assistance, as well concierge services.

Family-friendly benefits are policies and initiatives that help employees manage work and family responsibilities. Options may include parental leave with pay, flexible scheduling and remote employment.

Let's take a closer look at these benefits:

1 – Personal Services Benefits: Personal services include on-site childcare, concierge services and fitness centers that help employees manage their commitments and everyday activities.

2 – Family-Friendly Benefits: Paid parental leave, flexible scheduling and remote work alternatives are examples of family-friendly benefits that assist employees in combining work and family duties. Family-friendly benefits can help employees in managing the demands of motherhood and other caregiving duties while ensuring that they remain engaged and productive at work.

3 – Sick Child and Elder Care Benefits: Care for a sick child and care for an elderly individual are examples of family-friendly benefits supporting employees with caregiving duties.

4 – Educational Subsidies: Educational subsidies may include tuition reimbursement, training programs or opportunities for professional development that assist employees in advancing their professions.

5 – Domestic Partner Benefits: Employees with unmarried partners may access health insurance and other benefits through domestic partner benefits.

Flexible Benefits

As a type of employee benefits program, flexible benefits (also known as cafeteria plans or flexible spending accounts) give workers the freedom to select the perks they value most.

Cafeteria Benefits Plan

Employees participating in a cafeteria benefits plan can build their benefits strategy by selecting available services.

Health insurance, dental insurance, retirement savings programs and other benefit alternatives may all be available to employees under this system, in which the company provides a fixed amount of money or credits.

This method places the decision-making power for employee benefits squarely in the hands of the employees themselves, allowing them to tailor their benefits package to suit their requirements and preferences better.

Offering a variety of benefit alternatives and letting employees pick the perks that best suit their needs can help firms save money.

Flexible Work Schedules

A flexible work schedule plan aims to provide workers greater freedom in determining how long they put in each day. The possibilities are shorter workweeks, more flexible schedules, job sharing and remote work.

Employees can improve their work-life balance, stress levels and output with the help of these policies.

Section 4 – Employee Relations

Chapter 8: The Role of HR in Organizational Goals and Objectives

The HR department is responsible for achieving the short-term and long-term goals of an organization. It provides and maintains the organizational structure while effectively managing the employees.

In this chapter, we'll talk about the role of HR in setting and achieving organizational goals and objectives.

HR Policies, Procedures and Operations

HR policies, procedures and operations refer to the systems, rules and guidelines that govern how an organization manages its HR functions. This includes areas such as hiring, training, compensation, benefits, performance management, employee relations and more.

HR policies and procedures provide a framework for consistent and fair treatment of employees while also helping to ensure compliance with labor laws and regulations. Let's look at each in detail.

HR Policies

HR policies are guidelines adopted by the organization for managing its employees and handling issues within the company.

Almost all functions of HR management are covered within HR policies.

A good HR policy is easily understood, reasonably flexible, precise and related to the organization's objectives. These policies help with better control and coordination within the company while maintaining worker efficiency.

HR Procedures

HR procedures are guidelines that HR departments follow to manage various aspects of employee relations and administration. These procedures ensure consistent and fair treatment of employees and provide a clear understanding of HR policies and processes.

Some common HR procedures include:

- HR planning
- Recruitment
- Employee selection
- Hiring personnel
- Job-specific training
- Coordinating staff
- Working on employee relations
- Performance evaluation

The HR policy decides the action to be taken, and the procedure explains how it is supposed to be executed.

HR Operations

HR operations refer to the day-to-day tasks and activities that support the overall HR function. They support effective and efficient HR function management, ensuring that the organization's HR needs are met promptly and cost-effectively.

HR operations typically involve a range of processes, systems and tools that help to streamline HR activities and ensure that information is accurate, up to date and readily accessible to HR professionals.

Typical HR processes include:

- Managing employee records
- Benefits and processing payroll

- Performing background checks
- Carrying out employee onboarding
- Handling employee relations issues
- Management tasks

Organizational Goals and Objectives

Organizational objectives are short- and long-term plans a company creates for itself to fulfill its mission and vision.

Objectives are routine statements that illustrate what a business is looking to achieve, while goals assist a business in reaching its objectives.

For example, a business's goal may be to boost consumer satisfaction, while one of its objectives may be decreasing consumer complaints by 20 to 25% over the next six weeks. These objectives assist in balancing individual work with the overall direction of the company.

- Setting strong organizational objectives and goals is essential for:
- Supplying a crystal-clear path for the organization
- Promoting a sensation of purpose and motivation among employees
- Ensuring resources are used effectively
- Providing effective decision-making

Functions of HR Information System

HRIS is a program designed to assist with HR functions. Below are a number of the main capabilities of HRIS:

Data Management: HRIS helps businesses cope with worker information, job history, payroll information and benefits.

Search and Hiring: HRIS may help with recruiting and hiring process by enabling businesses to post job openings, monitor candidate information and tackle the work process.

Performance Management: HRIS can enable businesses to handle personnel performance by monitoring performance goals, providing feedback and coaching, as well as matching the performance appraisal process.

Learning Management: HRIS might help support personnel training and development by keeping track of employee training and development activities and offering access to instructional materials.

Compensation and Benefits Administration: HRIS can allow businesses to track employee compensation and benefits information by checking payroll information, managing employee benefits and supplying use of worker compensation reports.

Time and Attendance: HRIS keeps track of employee time-off requests, controlling tracking, computing and overtime hours worked.

Compliance: HRIS helps businesses stay compliant with HR-related laws by providing access to important HR-related information plus monitoring compliance with HR-associated procedures and policies.

Types of Organizational Structures and the Role of HR

The organizational method is the hierarchy of any firm's personnel. This framework incorporates workers' titles and their duties, along with crucial hierarchies.

Let's look at four types of organizational elements.

Functional Structure

In this kind of business, businesses are classified into teams with specific roles, such as finance, marketing, HR and others. Every division features a supervisor and is led by an administrator.

Advantages of such an arrangement include increased teamwork and higher efficacy in achieving results. The disadvantages include a lack of communication between departments and unhealthy competition, leading to losses.

Divisional Structure

Different teams or groups work together in this type of structure to reach a single goal. Each division has an executive who controls that group's budget and resources.

Benefits of the multidivisional structure include better service and centralized orders. The downside is poor integration with other branches and potential taxation.

Flatarchy

Companies with few employees use the flatarchy structure. It has no levels of management. The manager of the company is the bridge between the executives and employees.

Advantages of this structure include good communication, faster decision-making, increased cost-effectiveness and higher employee determination. The drawback is leadership confusion, which can lead to internal conflict.

Matrix Structure

In a matrix-style structure, employees are divided into teams that report to a functional and a product manager. Employees working for these companies have a wider skill set as they are assigned to different projects requiring a different level of expertise.

This structure creates a flexible work environment with open discussion. However, roles are not clearly defined and there may be conflict among the leadership.

Role of HR in Basic Organizational Communication

Organizational communication refers to communication between people working toward a common goal in the same workplace. Interaction between workers for the sake of conducting business or working toward an objective also falls under organizational communication.

There are several types of organizational communication, such as:

1 – Formal Communication: Formal communication uses a specific, predetermined format and structure. It includes official emails or job offers.

2 – Informal Communication: Also called grapevine communication, informal communication occurs through different social media or messaging apps. It doesn't have a specific format.

3 – Vertical Communication: This is communication that maintains a downward or upward hierarchy.

4 – Horizontal Communication: It doesn't require a communication flow, so employees talk to each other freely. It can include a conversation between two employees.

5 – Internal Communication: Conversations or communication within the company involving the company's employees or manager. For example, social activities within an organization.

6 – External Communication: External communication is the process through which a company communicates with the external world, such as a manager talking to clients or customers.

7 – Oral Communication: As the name indicates, the participants use verbal methods like face-to-face or over-the-phone to communicate with each other.

8 – Written Communication: It takes place in the written format. This type of communication often has delayed feedback, but it maintains a record for future reference, such as emails, letters and chats.

Methods Used by HR to Promote Organizational Communication

HR is responsible for managing the company and its employees while ensuring appropriate actions are taken for the organization's future. Let's look at the methods HR uses to promote organizational communication:

Give and Receive Feedback: Feedback in a positive environment has outstanding results. Employees realize their weaknesses and work on them to optimize their performance.

One-on-One Meetings: These develop coaching skills and are a good opportunity to build mutual respect. These meetings must be regular for them to yield positive results.

Active Listening: Active listening improves communication flow and the overall atmosphere of the company.

SWOT Analysis

SWOT stands for strengths, weaknesses, opportunities and threats. It helps assess the internal and external factors that affect a company.

The four components of a SWOT analysis are described below:

Strengths: These include things the company is good at, specific designs and qualities, internal resources and tangible assets.

Weaknesses: These include things the company lacks, things competitors are better at, resource limitations and unclear propositions.

Opportunities: These include underserved markets for specific products, fewer competitors in the area, the demand for the company's products and media coverage.

Threats: These include emerging competition, changing regulations, negative press coverage and changing customer attitudes.

How Does a SWOT Analysis Assist with Strategic Planning?

A SWOT analysis is a strategic planning model that identifies a company's strengths and areas for improvement. It helps organizations seize opportunities and prepare future strategies.

Strategic planning includes:

- Understanding a company's vision
- Assessing current position
- Determining priorities and objectives
- Defining responsibilities
- Measuring and evaluating results

A SWOT analysis comes in handy in the second step of strategic planning as it helps companies assess where they are. This helps with the organization's future planning to effectively achieve its goals.

Chapter 9: Employee Engagement and HR

Employee interaction plays an important role in creating a better work atmosphere. It's an essential driver in the success of a company.

HR plays a big role in making sure that workers are supplied with the proper resources, work environment and abilities for their jobs. Effective engagement methods increase productivity, decrease turnover, enhance work-customer human relationships and also affect the business's earnings.

In this chapter, we will discuss the importance, strategies and role of HR in promoting employee engagement.

The Employee Engagement Problem

Most problems arise not during the establishment of an engagement plan but after the plan has been implemented. Common issues that most companies overlook include:

Employee Retention

Hiring employees is not the only responsibility of HR. Recruiters also need to focus on retaining workers.

They can increase retention by creating an environment where employees feel valued. This can increase employee trust and engagement, leading to higher retention.

Employee Engagement

Although some effort is made to monitor employee engagement, annual surveys only provide a generalized perspective of the employees' experience. Performing more regular surveys can help companies overcome this issue.

Candidate Experience

Candidate experience and employee engagement are inseparable. The more positive the candidate's first impression of the recruiter, the higher the employee engagement levels.

Usually, companies do not take the time to make the candidate's first experience pleasant, which leaves a negative impression on the candidate and the company's reputation.

Companies can focus on creating a positive candidate experience to encourage engagement.

Resources for Employees

Companies need to make sure that all employees are well equipped/trained by tracking their progress throughout their projects.

What can HR do to Improve Employee Engagement?

HR plays a significant role in ensuring the success of the initiatives of employee engagement. It is the responsibility of HR to create, measure and evaluate policies that can attract good talent with the potential for growth and consistency.

Policies and steps that can be taken to help HR engage their employees with work include:

Increase Communication

A dedicated internal communication team can ensure that all departments of an organization stay connected as the organization grows.

As a company expands, different teams commonly start to work in isolation. To overcome this, HR can communicate openly with their employees, physically or digitally.

Remote and on-site teams can connect via digital platforms and access all upcoming updates, meeting schedules and more.

Promote Feedback

Feedback will assist personnel in enhancing their performance by offering them certain information on what they're succeeding in and what they need to improve.

When workers get feedback, they're more apt to comprehend what's expected from them.

Communicate the Organization's Vision

When workers comprehend the organization's mission, they are able to link their job to the larger picture, giving them a feeling of purpose. This enhances staff motivation and engagement.

Additionally, a common vision inspires personnel to look at the future and think of innovative solutions to issues. This may bring about innovation and improvement.

Empower Employees

Empowering workers involves providing them with the power, resources and independence to make choices and take steps that help the company's success. This strategy creates a feeling of ownership among workers, resulting in a better sense of dedication and determination.

If workers believe their viewpoints and actions matter, they're much more apt to become interested in the company's success.

How to Measure Employee Engagement

Employee engagement affects commitment, motivation and passion. It is a major driver of improved innovation, client satisfaction and financial success.

It is important for organizations to understand the various methods for measuring employee engagement and to adopt the most effective techniques to help them achieve their goals.

Let's look at some of the most common methods.

Stay Interviews

Stay interviews are conducted one-on-one with an employee and an employer. The employer directly asks employees about their interests and areas in which they need improvement.

The best way to conduct a stay interview is by:

- Informing the employee beforehand.
- Letting the employee know why the interview is being conducted.
- Providing a safe and comfortable environment to interview the employee.
- Asking appropriate and suitable questions.
- Thanking the employee for being a part of the organization and for his or her efforts.

Common questions that can be asked in a stay interview include:

- What makes you come to work every day?
- What do you like about working here?
- What do you dislike about working here?
- What would make your job more worthwhile?
- What can I do to support you?
- What might tempt you to leave this job?

Stay interviews are a great way to engage employees and assist them in identifying a problem in their careers at the initial stages.

Work/Life Balance Initiatives

Work/life balance initiatives are programs, policies and practices that organizations implement to help employees balance their work and personal lives.

Achieving a work/life balance has become increasingly important as people strive to achieve success in their careers while maintaining healthy personal lives.

Work/life balance initiatives can take many forms, such as:

Work-from-home Schemes

A work-from-home scheme may not be possible all the time, but allowing employees to work once or twice a week from home can help them maintain a good work/life balance.

Setting Boundaries

Certain boundaries can be set to ensure employees are not sacrificing personal time. These boundaries need to be set by the employer and can include the following:

1. Denying access to the office after a certain hour.
2. Informing clients of acceptable call hours and work schedules.
3. Requiring that work phones and computers are left at the office during vacations.
4. Informing employees not to respond to work calls and emails outside work hours.

Providing Family-friendly Policies

These policies include different activities to help employees with their personal lives. Examples include providing on-site day care, "bring your child to work" day, remote working for employees with sick relatives and other initiatives.

Alternative Work Arrangements

Alternate work arrangements include different positions in which employees can work, such as:

Job Sharing: In this arrangement, multiple employees share one position at different times. Part-time workers may also be included in job sharing.

Telecommuting: Working from any site other than the office is known as telecommuting. Telecommuting arrangements are reviewed by the department's HR consultant for consistency and tracking. They can help optimize workload and promote a healthy work/life balance.

Flexible Working Arrangements

Flexible work arrangements can help employees manage work and non-work-related activities without running into health problems. These arrangements can be of many types. Some of them include:

Hybrid Work: A work environment in which some employees work on-site and some work remotely is known as a hybrid workplace. The type of work assigned to employees will be based on circumstances, objectives and personal preferences. Hybrid work prioritizes how employees work instead of where they work.

Condensed Workweek: Unlike the usual five days per week, a condensed workweek concentrates on working the same time for a lesser number of days every week. Probably the most prevalent kind of condensed workweek is usually a four-day workweek instead of a five-day one.

Flextime: In this arrangement, employees can choose their work hours as long as they complete the required contracted hours.

Shift Work: An arrangement in which work is divided into shifts, morning and evening or morning and night, is called shift work. Employers benefit from this arrangement as work continues day and night.

The key is determining which work arrangements will provide sufficient flexibility to keep employees happy without negatively impacting productivity or work quality.

Remote Working

Remote work can be done anywhere and excludes physical attendance from the workplace. Often, companies employing remote workers will have staff located in different countries.

Remote workers are not required to attend team-building sessions or office-based meetings but may be connected to the organization by video conference.

Employee Recognition Programs

Employee recognition systems help identify worthy staff members in a business. These workers are compensated based on their performance and achievements.

Awards can be given to the employees through gift cards, certificates, outings and other incentives. Some awards include:

- Customer service awards
- Employee appreciation awards
- Employee recognition walls
- Weekly social media shoutouts

Implementing an Employee Engagement Program

The steps to implementing an employee engagement program include the following:

1. Ensure the employee engagement plan aligns with the organization's vision, values and goals.
2. Create a respective leadership team that makes sure that the plan is set accordingly and is being followed.
3. Allocate budgetary resources.

4. Effectively communicate the plan to the employers and the employees.
5. Review and report on progress regularly.
6. Make changes to the engagement plan when it seems necessary.
7. Develop an organizational culture that supports the strategy.

Case Study: Improving Employee Engagement

Employee engagement is essential for improving a company's productivity, employee retention, profitability and customer service. Let's look at a case study to understand how employee engagement correlates with organizational success.

The following case study was conducted by AkzoNobel Paint and Coatings Companies. AkzoNobel is a multinational company creating paints and performance coatings for industry and consumers worldwide.

The company is committed to chief excellence and providing Tomorrow's Answers Today™.

Purpose

The purpose of the study was to figure out:

- If the employees were satisfied with current working conditions.
- What change could occur if the employees were to work together?
- Whether or not employees felt connected with other people in the organization.

Three viewpoint surveys were conducted annually by Gallup in AkzoNobel in 2010. They were based on 12 questions about the organization's progress, identifying areas that needed improvement.

The surveys allowed HR employees to freely voice their opinions regarding their current work environment and how they could work together to effect change.

Besides the Q12, Gallup also introduced a Viewpoint Employee Engagement program by incorporating customer focus, entrepreneurial thinking, integrity and responsibility into developing talents.

Findings

The data collected in the surveys found that the overall engagement score of the corporate workforce was 3.81, and of corporate HR was 3.56.

The survey indicated no difference in the data collected between 2011 and 2012. This means that no initiative was taken to improve employee engagement.

Another survey was conducted in May 2012, which showed a slight improvement in overall engagement scores, from 3.74 to 3.80.

Problem

The main problem that arose after looking at the data and surveys was that even though the surveys were being conducted, there was no action taken to improve the engagement.

Employees felt disconnected from the organization and wanted more than just a pat on the back when it came to getting praised by their managers.

Research Questions and Approach

The case study was used to investigate the phenomenon of low employee engagement in AkzoNobel. The research question was answered by the following methods:

1. Reviewing research literature, as a theoretical foundation, based on the importance of employee engagement.
2. Conducting structured interviews in corporate HR and analyzing the data.
3. Analyzing the engagement survey as secondary data.

4. Conducting quantitative analysis to answer the research question.

5. Providing solutions to the arising problem.

6. Checking the feasibility of the provided solution and asking employees for feedback.

Post-hoc Analysis

Lunch and learning sessions were introduced after the survey conducted in 2013, where it was inferred that the employees wanted to work together as one AkzoNobel. They also wished to have more freedom and authority to make autonomous decisions.

Moreover, they wanted their suggestions to be listened to and for them to bring a change in the old ways of the organization.

Discussion

The research work confirmed that managers played a significant role in employee engagement. Many differences were found in the managers' self-image and employees' perception of job autonomy, work-person fit and development support, all of which significantly impacted employee engagement.

Managers expected employees to proactively take charge of their development and ask for development opportunities. Employees believed it to be the managers' responsibility to encourage employees, especially when the manager was an HR professional.

Employees wanted challenges that could help them utilize their talents. They wanted to be trusted and supported to make better use of their ideas. However, their managers didn't realize this was an issue.

Conclusion

Employees feel disengaged when they are not given opportunities to develop and utilize their skills and knowledge meaningfully. This disengagement can arise when managers do not support their employees' decisions, leading to frustration and a lack of motivation to take on new challenges.

Oftentimes, workers are prepared to undertake new jobs that permit them to put their skills to use, though they might not be offered an opportunity to do so. This may lead to a decrease in efficiency and all-around job satisfaction.

Recommendations

The achievements of engagement programs are determined by how engaged supervisors are because this has an immediate influence on staff members. Therefore, to enhance employee engagement, executives and supervisors have to take a decisive role as role models within the company.

A great way to promote employee involvement is to motivate workers by offering them a stake in their job and by permitting them to undertake tasks that match their abilities and expertise.

Plus, supervisors can establish particular, measurable, achievable and time-bound team goals which are tough but doable. This helps workers feel a sense of purpose.

Concurrent feedback and communication between supervisors and staff members can also be essential to preserving engagement. Managers might keep a management diary to record progress and provide frequent feedback to staff members. Similarly, workers are able to offer feedback to their supervisors, which will help better their performance and develop a feeling of accountability.

To make sure that everybody is on the same page, a common HR calendar with future functions, group meetings and due dates can be put into action. This can enable supervisors to delegate duties and tasks to the most appropriate staff members, helping them to optimize their potential.

Chapter 10: Performance Management and Appraisal

A crucial part of HRM is performance management and appraisal. It helps ensure employees are meeting performance standards, discovering areas for growth and ensuring their work aligns with the organization's goals and objectives.

Setting performance goals, offering regular feedback and carrying out formal evaluations are all parts of an ongoing process called effective PM. Giving workers the freedom to direct their growth and giving managers the information they need to make career decisions fosters a high-performance culture.

In this chapter, we'll cover the essential elements of performance management and appraisal, such as performance objectives, setting targets, giving feedback, administering formal evaluations and more.

What is a Performance Appraisal?

A person's work performance and impact on the business are routinely assessed through performance reviews. These may, in addition, be utilized to determine if pay should be increased or complemented with a different kind of incentive.

An effective performance assessment gives workers feedback on their effectiveness, determines areas for growth and creates brand-new performance objectives for the long term.

An assessment of a worker's overall performance usually involves a review of the work description, talking about performance objectives and evaluating the individual's capabilities, achievements and overall worth to the business.

The process might consist of a self-assessment by the person, an appraisal by the manager or supervisor and comments from other parties, such as coworkers or clients.

The Performance Appraisal Process

A planned evaluation of a worker's overall job performance is known as a performance appraisal. It is generally completed semi-annually or annually to find out how workers are attaining their objectives and goals.

There are several steps involved in this process, including:

Planning and Goal Setting

The manager and worker collaborate to develop performance goals for the coming season. This stage creates the structure for the subsequent phases of the evaluation and ensures that everybody is conscious of what's anticipated.

Ongoing Feedback

The management regularly updates employees on their performance and growth throughout the year. This assists employees in remaining focused and resolving any problems as soon as they arise.

Performance Documentation

Throughout the year, the management keeps track of the employees' performance. This is known as performance documentation and can include meeting notes, emails and other types of interactions.

Appraisal Preparation

Managers review performance records and prepare for the official appraisal meeting. They can seek advice from other managers or HR experts at this stage to gain more information.

Appraisal Meeting

A manager typically holds an appraisal meeting to discuss an employee's performance. These typically occur every three to six months and serve as an opportunity for the employees to examine their goals and objectives and discuss their aspirations.

Review and Follow-up

Following the appraisal meeting, the manager and employee discuss the appraisal and pinpoint any improvement areas. Management can also offer further coaching or training to assist the employees in reaching certain objectives.

Defining Employee Goals and Performance Standards

Setting specific objectives and performance benchmarks for workers is the first step in the performance appraisal process. These objectives and benchmarks must be specific, measurable, achievable, relevant and timely (SMART).

The employees should work with management to design these goals, taking into account the organization's goals, strengths and weaknesses.

Employee goals can include increasing sales by a certain percentage, decreasing customer complaints, increasing data entry accuracy or finishing a training course.

Performance standards might include attendance, punctuality, teamwork or customer service expectations.

Standards and goals should be clear and practical for employees. Also, routinely checking in with employees during the appraisal period helps ensure that objectives are being reached.

Who Should Perform the Appraisal?

Depending on the organization's policies and procedures, a specific person is assigned to do the appraisal. The individual who does the appraisal is typically the employees' manager or supervisor.

In most cases, the employees' performance is reviewed, feedback is given and the supervisor or manager sets expectations.

Peers, subordinates and customers are just a few of the various raters that some firms may use during the evaluation process. This kind of 360-degree feedback provides a more thorough assessment of a worker's performance.

Traditional Tools for Appraising Performance

Traditional tools for appraising performance assess an employee's performance on the job. These techniques offer a systematic and uniform manner of performance evaluation.

They include:

Graphic Rating Scale Method

With the graphic rating scale approach, the employee's performance is graded in relation to each level of a rating scale with numerous performance levels. This can cover things like job expertise, work quality and attendance.

For instance, a worker might receive ratings of "above average" for job knowledge, "average" for work quality and "below average" for attendance.

Alternation Ranking Method

The employee is ranked in relation to others holding the same position using this method. For example, a worker might be rated as the second-best performer in a department of ten people.

Forced Distribution Method

With the forced distribution approach, ratings are assigned per a specified distribution, such as 10% of employees receiving outstanding ratings, 20% receiving above-average ratings and so on.

Even if some employees receive ratings that are lower than they should, the appraiser must then put each employee into the appropriate categories.

Critical Incident Method

The critical incident method entails identifying certain instances of employee behavior that have had a major negative influence on the job. These instances, whether favorable or unfavorable, are utilized to gauge the employee's performance.

Narrative Forms Method

This approach involves the appraiser writing a narrative outlining the employee's performance. Although this method can yield more detailed information, it can be time-consuming and arbitrary.

Behaviorally Anchored Rating Scales

This instrument gauges employee performance by measuring them according to predefined behavioral patterns. These patterns can include behaviors like "the employee doesn't make eye contact with the customer" or "the employee asks the customer many questions."

Typically, a vertical scale with ratings from five to nine depicts performance levels from very poor to excellent.

Management by Objectives

The management-by-objectives approach entails setting employees' performance standards based on their capacity to reach defined, measurable goals.

Electronic Performance Monitoring

The electronic performance technique involves tracking an employee's performance in real-time, utilizing technology like time and attendance systems. However, although it can give a more accurate view of a worker's performance, it also raises privacy issues.

Conversation Days

The conversation days approach entails planning routine, casual conversations between staff members and supervisors to review performance and offer feedback. This can establish a cooperative relationship between managers and employees.

What is Customized Talent Management?

To manage the performance and growth of their employees, organizations use customized talent management, which consists of several strategies and methodologies. These can include talent development, career management, remuneration and performance management, all of which work together to match an organization's human capital with its objectives.

By developing a personalized strategy that addresses the particular requirements of the organization, customized talent management aims to draw in, keep and inspire top talent. This tailored strategy ensures that employees have the skills and competencies essential to meet corporate objectives by taking into account the organization's culture, industry, size and other aspects.

For instance, a technology corporation might design a tailored talent management strategy centered on staff training and development initiatives to keep up with the quickly evolving state of technology.

So, by implementing a tailored talent management strategy, a business can enhance worker performance, raise job satisfaction and promote a healthy workplace culture. As a result, businesses experience better results, make more revenue and, thus, gain a competitive advantage.

Common Errors with Rater Error Appraisal Problems

In performance management, it's crucial to identify and address potential issues using the appraisal process. Here are a few key points to consider:

Potential Rating Problems

Potential rating problems include rating errors, halo effects and central tendency bias:

Rating Errors: These refer to when the appraiser rates an employee based on performance on a single task rather than considering overall performance.

Halo Effects: These occur when the appraiser is influenced by a single characteristic of the employee, such as likability, rather than evaluating job performance objectively.

Central Tendency Bias: This refers to when the appraiser gives most employees average ratings rather than reflecting the true range of performance.

The Problem of Bias

Bias can develop when the appraiser has predetermined notions about the employees, their performance or their potential. Race, gender, close friendships or religion may be the reason for such discrimination.

To avoid bias, the appraiser must be trained in impartial, objective appraisal techniques.

The Need for Fairness

The employee and the appraiser must feel that the procedure was fair. In other words, the appraiser must assess performance using consistent, objective standards and give the employee clear and useful feedback.

Organizations can increase the precision and use of the performance management system by avoiding mistakes and ensuring fairness.

Appraising Performance: The Law

The legal structure governing performance reviews can be complicated, with various rules and laws applying based on the kind of business, how many employees they have and where they are located.

When conducting performance reviews, firms must abide by several important rules and regulations discussed earlier in the book. These include Title VII of the Civil Rights Act of 1964, ADA and ADEA.

Managing the Appraisal Interview

The appraisal interview is a critical part of the performance appraisal process. To conduct an effective appraisal interview, it's important to:

- Prepare beforehand.
- Create a supportive and nonthreatening atmosphere.
- Listen actively to the employee.
- Provide specific feedback.
- Offer concrete suggestions for improvement.

Conducting the Appraisal Interview

A crucial step in the performance appraisal process is the interview. The manager must gather all relevant details before the interview and establish definite meeting objectives.

Also, the manager should actively listen during the interview, ask open-ended questions and offer helpful criticism. It's critical to foster a welcoming workplace where employees feel free to express their ideas.

Handling a Defensive Subordinate

When doing the assessment interview, employees frequently feel defensive. To counteract this, the manager should discuss the subject with understanding and empathy.

Supervisors should refrain from criticizing or condemning their employees and place greater emphasis on educating them about how their behavior affects their output. It is also critical that managers offer employees constructive criticism and specific examples to assist them in growing.

Criticizing a Subordinate

It can be challenging to criticize subordinates, but it is a necessary step in reviewing their work.

The manager should constructively handle criticism and give specific instances where employees need to improve. They must also be supportive and instructive to assist workers in achieving their goals.

Handling a Written Warning

Occasionally, a written warning from the performance review process may be issued.

The best course of action for managers in this circumstance is to handle it sympathetically, explain what has to be improved and give concrete examples.

What is Performance Management?

Performance management is a systematic strategy for overseeing and enhancing employee performance to achieve corporate and personal objectives. It entails establishing clear performance objectives, keeping track of and assessing workers' advancement, giving feedback and support and deciding on possibilities for recognition, incentives and professional growth.

By coordinating individual efforts with the organization's mission, goals and objectives, performance management aims to increase overall organizational performance.

Performance management needs to be included in an organization's entire culture and strategy for success. To achieve this, senior leadership must support it and buy into it. Performance objectives and criteria must be communicated, and managers and staff must have continual chances for training and development.

Total Quality Management and Performance Appraisal

Total quality management (TQM) is a continuous improvement technique used to improve the goods and services offered by a firm by involving every employee in the process. It applies to many organizational tasks, including performance evaluation.

Performance evaluations are a crucial component of TQM since they enable firms to evaluate employee performance and pinpoint areas for development. Organizations can boost overall performance by establishing a culture of continuous improvement by implementing TQM principles in performance appraisal.

Customer focus, meeting customers' wants and expectations, is one of the fundamental tenets of TQM. By making sure that employees are assessed based on their capacity to satisfy consumer wants and provide high-quality goods and services, this approach can be used to improve performance evaluation.

Another important principle is continuous improvement, which directs businesses to look for ways to constantly enhance their operations. It uses regular performance reviews to discover areas for development and execute changes that will improve employee performance.

Chapter 11: Building Positive Employee Relations

An essential part of managing HR is fostering good employee relations. It entails establishing and preserving an environment at work that encourages employees to be successful and satisfied.

Aspects of employee relations include managing conflict and resolving disagreements that could occur at work. Employees are more likely to feel appreciated, valued and inspired to do their best work when disagreements are addressed and resolved immediately.

Additionally, employee morale can be increased and turnover rates can be lowered with excellent employee relationships. These components provide a climate in the workplace that is both more lucrative and effective. Conversely, a hostile workplace atmosphere and high turnover rates could be the outcome of bad worker interactions.

In this section, we will look at the primary components of creating positive employee associations at work and investigate methods for successful communication.

What Are Employee Relations?

Employee relations are the interactions and ties between workers and the company or the business they're a part of.

Developing a good work environment and supporting worker well-being is crucial for better business results as well as the firm's overall performance, which may improve employee satisfaction.

The following are just a few of the duties and activities that fall under the umbrella of employee relations:

- Maintaining open and transparent communication channels between employees and management.
- Addressing employee concerns and complaints in a fair and timely manner.
- Providing opportunities for employee involvement and feedback.
- Promoting job satisfaction and motivation through fair compensation, benefits and opportunities for growth and development.
- Encouraging collaboration and teamwork among employees.
- Implementing programs and policies to promote workplace diversity, equity and inclusion.

How to Build Positive Employee Relations

Employees must be treated fairly; bullying and victimization must be reduced and productive communication and involvement initiatives must be used to maintain a productive and healthy work environment.

Let's look at some methods for fostering good employee relations.

Ensuring Fair Treatment

No matter their position or level of seniority, fairly treating all employees means treating them with respect and equality. It also entails giving all employees an equitable wage in exchange for work and offering them equal opportunities for growth, training and career advancement.

Decreasing Bullying and Victimization

Setting clear expectations for how employees should behave is one of the simplest methods to prevent workplace bullying. If employers uphold a solid set of corporate values, employees will respect one another according to these principles.

By encouraging positive interpersonal dynamics and keeping an eye on employee behavior, managers should set an excellent example for their teams. However, while setting expectations, managers must prevent ambiguity.

Using Communications Programs

The foundation of good employee relations is effective communication. This could include conducting regular meetings with staff, promoting direct and honest communication and giving assistance and support wherever needed.

Developing Employee Recognition/Relations Programs

Employee relations and recognition initiatives are created to thank employees for their efforts and services to the business.

These can consist of consistent bonuses, promotions and other types of recognition, such as employee of the month awards.

Utilizing Employee Involvement Programs

Participating in decision-making through employee participation programs allows employees to provide ideas for enhancing the workplace or participating in team-building exercises.

Companies may promote a feeling of responsibility and ownership in workers by involving them in the work process, enhancing their motivation and job satisfaction.

Features of an Ethical Organization

When making decisions and performing everyday duties, an ethical organization prioritizes ethical principles and values. At work, ethical and moral norms are upheld and employees are treated with respect.

Employees, clients and the community all respect businesses that handle themselves ethically. Some of the characteristics of an ethical organization may include the following:

Clear Ethical Guidelines

The company should be guided by a clear set of moral principles that define proper conduct and how decisions should be made.

Ethical Leadership

Ethical leadership creates a positive ethical culture, setting the organization's tone. So, leaders should exemplify moral conduct and inspire others to do likewise.

Open and Transparent Communication

In ethical firms, it is very important to have a proper communication network between staff, management and stakeholders. This promotes trust and a positive workplace atmosphere.

Employee Training

Employees should receive ethical decision-making and conduct training from their employers. This promotes ethical behavior in the workforce.

Holding Employees Accountable

Employees should be accountable for their activities in an organization, including ethical behavior. This safeguards the company's integrity and ensures workers act honorably and responsibly.

Encouraging Reporting of Unethical Behavior

An ethical organization should encourage employees to report unethical behavior and support those who do. This helps to identify and resolve ethical issues and to create a culture of transparency and trust.

Ethics and Employee Rights

Businesses need an obvious code of ethics to determine expectations for decision-making and conduct among managers and staff members. This code needs to address issues such as professional conduct at the office, secrecy and sincerity. It should be in line with the company's ideas.

Employers are accountable for ensuring that employees know their rights and creating practices and policies to encourage those rights. Developing reporting systems and working with moral or worker rights violations is a part of this.

The overall success of the business can be impacted favorably by creating a robust ethical and worker rights tradition. It can improve management's reliability, help make workers happier and reduce turnover.

What Shapes Ethical Behavior at the Office

To keep an ethical workplace, it is vital that you know the different elements which shape ethical behavior. Here are a few of the major elements which can affect moral behavior at work:

Leadership

The behavior and actions of leaders can have a substantial effect on the moral environment of a company.

Leaders who model good behavior and hold their personnel accountable for their actions will probably have an effect on ethics at work.

Employee Motivation

Employees motivated by job satisfaction, recognition and a sense of purpose are more likely to exhibit ethical behavior at work.

Personal Values and Beliefs

Personal values and beliefs can influence ethical behavior, as employees may act according to their principles.

Pressure From Colleagues or Superiors

Social pressure from coworkers or superiors can affect good conduct at work. This could include pressure in order to adhere to the standards of the company, to meet particular performance goals or to keep good relationships with other people.

How Can HR Managers Create an Ethical Environment?

A moral workplace environment is vital for developing good employee relationships.

HR managers play an important role in establishing and maintaining such an environment. Some of the key strategies they can use to create an ethical environment include:

- Defining and communicating ethical standards
- Providing ethics training
- Encouraging an open-door policy
- Modeling ethical behavior

How to Manage Employee Discipline

Employee discipline comprises applying rules, regulations and procedures. It aims to correct improper behavior, such as misconduct or subpar performance, and to stop the recurrence of such problems.

Effectively managing employee discipline can reduce the danger of legal and financial ramifications, maintain a productive and healthy work environment and guarantee that employees are fulfilling their job tasks.

Organizations must set and effectively communicate clear norms and expectations for employee behavior to handle employee punishment. This can be accomplished by writing employee handbooks, rules and procedures manuals and other material that clearly defines acceptable behavior and the repercussions for disobeying it.

The Pillar of Fair Discipline

When disciplinary action is required, it is crucial to follow a fair and consistent procedure that enables staff members to comprehend what they did incorrectly, what they should do differently and the consequences of continuing noncompliance.

Disciplinary measures might include everything from written or verbal warnings to termination of employment, depending on the severity of the infraction.

Discipline in the Workplace: Females vs. Males

Regardless of gender, all employees should be subject to the same level of discipline at work. Nonetheless, research suggests there can be some gender bias in how punishment is applied in the workplace.

According to research, men are more likely to face disciplinary action for objective reasons, such as performance. Women are more likely to face disciplinary action for subjective reasons, such as attitude. Unconscious bias or gender roles and behavior stereotypes can be blamed for this.

Women can also encounter more obstacles when reporting incidents of harassment or discrimination at work, which might prevent the offender from being punished or disciplined. This might lead to a culture of unfairness and inequality, which could have detrimental effects on the employee's performance.

In order to remedy these issues, businesses must have clear, uniform procedures and rules for coping with workplace behavior and discipline. Discipline programs skewed toward females may be reduced by education and training on unconscious bias, diversity and addition.

Furthermore, promoting open dialogue and respect can help stop cases of discrimination and harassment, which may lead to a fair and equal disciplinary process for every person on the staff.

How to Discipline an Employee

Disciplining workers is a tough undertaking for HR managers. The main element of effective discipline is approaching it in a positive fashion that can assist staff members in seeing the effect of their behavior and boost their overall performance.

Here are a few steps for personnel discipline:

Create Clear Rules: The initial step in dealing with employee discipline involves establishing specific regulations, policies and treatments that all staff members understand.

Consistent Enforcement: It's vital that you follow the rules regularly and fairly. Be certain that disciplinary measures are taken immediately and regularly whenever violations occur. This can help to build a lifestyle of accountability and self-discipline at the office.

Document Incidents: Document disciplinary situations and keep comprehensive records.

Give Feedback: Give feedback to workers regarding their effectiveness and actions. Provide solid criticism on what they're succeeding in and what they have to improve on.

Use Progressive Discipline: Use progressive discipline, starting with verbal warnings, then written warnings, suspension and termination if necessary.

Investigate Thoroughly: Before taking any disciplinary action, conduct a thorough investigation to ensure the facts are correct and that all parties have been heard.

Maintain Confidentiality: Maintaining confidentiality throughout the disciplinary process is essential to protect employees' privacy and prevent rumors from spreading. Share information only with those who have a legitimate need to know.

Provide Support: Support employees struggling with performance or behavior issues. Offer resources such as coaching, training or counseling to help them improve their performance or address personal issues affecting their work.

Section 5 – Compliance and Risk Management

Chapter 12: US Laws and Regulations for Businesses

A business comprises all profit-seeking activities that provide goods and services necessary to an economic system. Every country has its own set of laws about business, which are to be acknowledged and followed if a company or enterprise is to thrive.

These laws and regulations benefit employers and employees and collectively build the country's economy. In this chapter, we will discuss the laws specifically affecting businesses, agencies, employers and employees.

Importance of Employment Law

Employment laws protect workers from exploitation and wrongdoing by their employers. They include laws regarding wages, workplace safety, compensation and retirement.

The primary purpose of employment laws is to maintain a healthy balance in the workplace while protecting the rights of the company's employers and workers. They provide legislation on salary, discrimination, leaves and many other work-related aspects.

Laws for One or More Employees

The Consumer Credit Protection Act

This act was passed in 1968. Before this law, consumers in the US didn't have any rights. Lenders did not have to disclose loan terms and could charge atrocious interest rates.

The act's purpose was to protect consumers from abusive practices. It affected banks, debt collectors, credit card issuers and more. The law has the following aspects:

- **The Truth in the Lending Act** ensures that creditors provide complete information about the transaction.
- **The Fair Credit Reporting Act** regulates credit reports.
- **The Fair Debt Collection Act** establishes rules and restrictions for debt collectors.
- **The Equal Credit Opportunity Act** prevents creditors from discriminating.
- **The Electronic Fund Transfer Act** protects consumers' finances while making electronic or online transactions.

The Copeland "Anti-kickback" Act

This act was approved in 1934. It called for vendors to pay all due earnings and provide weekly compliance reports. It also prevented contractors from demanding bonuses from staff.

The Davis-Bacon Act

In 1931, the Davis-Bacon Act went into law, with modifications taking effect in 2002. The statute guarantees that workers and mechanics get local standard salaries on public works or projects.

Specifically, it applies to contractors and subcontractors working on the construction, alteration or repair of public buildings or works that are federally funded or assisted and which exceed $2,000. The act sets a minimum hourly wage rate for workers, providing them with fair compensation for their labor.

The Dodd-Frank Wall Street Reform and Consumer Protection Act

The act was passed after the 2008 financial crisis and enacted in 2010. Its purpose was to promote financial stability by improving transparency in the financial system and protecting consumers from abusive financial deals.

It aimed to increase the government's oversight of trading in complex financial instruments. The restrictions were placed on proprietary trading, which financial institutions were allowed to practice. These were intended to prevent the collapse of major financial institutions.

The Electronics Communications Privacy Act (ECPA) 1986

The law governs third-party interceptions of electronic or online communications. ECPA makes it illegal for any individual, the police or the government to intentionally intercept, access or disclose any wire oral or electronic communication.

This can only be done through proper authorization, such as obtaining a search warrant or consent from the recipient and if there is any suspicion of criminal activity.

The Employee Polygraph Protection Act (1988)

The act prohibits most private employers from using lie detector tests for pre-employment screening or during employment. Employers are also prohibited from discriminating against employees who refuse such tests under this act. Federal, state and local governments are exempted from this law.

However, the federal government can conduct lie detector tests for individuals engaged in national security-related activities. Polygraph testing can also be carried out in private firms if a workplace incident results in financial loss.

The Employee Retirement Income Security Act (ERISA) 1974

This is a federal state law that sets minimum standards for most retirement plans and establishes protection for consumers, including standards about disclosing plan information and rules regarding fiduciary responsibilities for the plans.

The act also contains rules about the federal income tax effects of transactions associated with employee benefit plans. Moreover, ERISA protects retirement savings from mismanagement and abuse while clarifying that those in charge of those savings must act in the participants' best interests.

The Equal Pay Act (1963)

The law was designed to abolish pay discrimination based on gender and wage disparities between the sexes. This had been an amendment to the Fair Labor Standard Act, ratified by John F. Kennedy.

Regardless of gender, the EPA protects everyone equally. It covers all forms of compensation, such as bonuses, insurance, salary, paid holidays, along with other benefits.

The Fair and Accurate Credit Transactions Act (FACT)

FACT was passed in 2003 as an amendment to the Fair Credit Reporting Act, adding provisions to improve the accuracy of consumers' credit records. Consumers are allowed to obtain a free copy of their credit files from reporting agencies once a year.

The Fair Reporting Credit Act (FRCA)

FRCA is a federal statute that regulates the collection of credit information and credit reports. It was passed to deal with the truthfulness of the personal data supplied in the documents of credit reporting companies.

The FCRA regulates users of consumer reports, furnishers of consumer information and consumer reporting agencies. Along with the Fair Debt Collection Practices Act (FDCPA), FRCA forms the foundation of consumer rights law in the United States.

The Foreign Corrupt Practices Act (FCPA)

The FCPA prohibits any payout to foreign officials, including anything of value or intending to acquire or retain business. It was created as an anti-bribery law in the aftermath of corrupt financial practices and illegal payments.

The law is administered by the US Department of Justice and the Securities and Exchange Commission. Under this law, it is illegal to consent to the demands of government officials to donate to a charity or political fund which is not constituted under the law of the land.

The Health Information Technology for Economic and Clinical Health (HITECH) Act

This law affects the health care system by promoting the use and adoption of health information technology.

It established the Office of National Coordinator for Health Information Technology within the Department of Health and Human Services (HHS). The purpose of HITECH was to:

- Improve medical quality.
- Protect public safety through early detection and swift response to infectious diseases.
- Lower the price of health care.
- Encourage prevention, early detection and control associated with chronic illness.
- Facilitate medical research.
- Secure patients' health data.

The Health Insurance Portability and Accountability Act (HIPAA) 1996

HIPAA was developed to establish national standards to safeguard sensitive patient information concerning their overall health from being divulged with no knowledge or consent of the affected person.

The act guarantees that individuals can shift from one health plan to another without losing coverage or being denied insurance due to pre-existing conditions. It ensures patient confidentiality, keeps track of disclosed information, and in case of a significant information breach, HHS is notified within 60 days.

The Immigration and Nationality Act (INA) 1952

Under this law, employers can only hire people who may legally work in the US, so foreigners need to be authorized to work in the US. An individual's identity and employment eligibility must be verified before hiring.

The Immigration Reform and Control Act (IRCA) 1986

According to IRCA, hired employees must demonstrate work eligibility by filling out forms and submitting certifications of work authorization.

The IRS Intermediate Sanctions (2002)

Intermediate sanctions are penalties the IRS can impose on an individual involved in an excessively beneficial transaction. An excess benefit transaction is where a nonprofit organization pays more or receives less than fair market value.

The most common form of excess benefit transaction involves unreasonable compensation for services.

The Labor Management Relations Act (LMRA) 1947

The LMRA restricts the power of labor unions and their activities. It lists activities inhibited by labor unions, such as secondary boycotts, coercion or discrimination and the influence of employees' decisions to participate or refrain from union activities.

The act guarantees employees bargaining rights and denies supervisors legal protection if they organize their unions. It also prohibits closed shops and unfair union labor practices.

The Labor-Management Reporting and Disclosure Act (1959)

This law regulates the internal affairs of the labor union. It protects union members' rights and ensures unions run smoothly and democratically.

It requires regular elections for union officials by secret ballot. Under this law, ex-convicts and communists are prohibited from holding union office.

The National Labor Relations Act (NLRA) 1935

The NLRA guarantees the right of private sector employees to organize into trade unions and engage in bargaining and strikes.

The primary purpose of the NLRA is to protect the rights of employees, encourage collective bargaining and limit certain private-sector labor and management practices that could potentially harm the workers or the economy.

This act also forbids employers from interfering with employees organizing, forming or assisting a labor organization or from working together to improve the conditions of employment.

The Norris-LaGuardia Act

This act, which will be discussed in more depth later in the book, outlaws yellow-dog contracts in which employees agree not to participate in any labor union. It also extends legal protection to peaceful strikes, picketing and boycotts.

The court's power is restricted in the issue of injunctions against unions engaged in peaceful strikes. Each employee is guaranteed the right to bargain freely without restraint or interference, so much so that collective bargaining is considered a matter of public policy.

The Occupational Safety and Health Act (OSHA) 1970

This law was implemented to ensure safe and healthy conditions for working men and women. It has three main objectives:

- Recognize hazards in the workplace.
- Identify and correct the risks.
- Plan and implement safe work practices.

The Pension Protection Act (PPA) 2006

This law was designed to improve pension and retirement plans. It protects retirement accounts and holds companies' underfunded pension accounts accountable.

The PPA also strengthened the overall pension system. Under this legislation, enrolling employees in 401(k) plans became easier.

The Portal-to-Portal Act (1947)

This law clarifies employers' responsibility and adds protection for employees to ensure they are paid for all their work time.

It gives employers the autonomy to not pay their employees for their time on preliminary and concluding activities—activities performed for which they weren't employed.

The Rehabilitation Act (1973)

This law was enacted to provide equal access to disabled people by removing transportation, employment and architectural barriers.

It prohibits discrimination based on disability in federal government programs and federal contractors' employment practices.

The Retirement Equity Act (REA)

This act requires employers and companies to count all services since the age of 18 while determining retirement benefits and all earnings since the age of 21, even if there are breaks in service up to five years. It applies to all genders.

This law also states that pension benefits are considered joint assets while working on a divorce settlement. It recognizes maternity and paternity leave.

The Revenue Act (1978)

This act reduced individual income taxes and increased the personal tax exemption from $750 to $1,000. Corporate tax rates were also reduced from 48% to 46%.

The Revenue Act eliminated the requirement that an individual maintain a US residence to be eligible for the earned income credit.

The Service Contract Act (1965)

This act provides for minimum wages and fringe benefits as well as other conditions of work under service contracts.

A service contract directly engages the time and effort of the contractor, whose purpose is to perform an identifiable task. It can be personal or non-personal and may cover an individual or an organization.

The law created labor standards for certain persons employed by federal contractors to serve federal agencies. Under this act, service employees are prohibited from performing unsanitary or hazardous tasks that are dangerous to the health of the employees.

The Small Business Job Protection Act (1996)

This act is designed to increase the competitiveness of small businesses. It simplifies pension rules, lowers taxes for small businesses and adjusts minimum wages.

It declares that the government should aid and assist the interest of small businesses. Moreover, this law provides flexibility to employers in complying with minimum wage and overtime requirements.

The Social Security Act (1935)

The SSA contains three major components:

- Insurance for old age
- Compensation for unemployed individuals
- Provision of aid for families with disabled individuals and children

This act also benefits victims of industrial accidents. Moreover, it provides general welfare to the individuals mentioned above. A social security board exists on both federal and state levels.

The Tax Reform Act (1986)

The main features of the act include:

- Tax relief for the poor
- Reduction in tax rates
- Shifting to corporate taxes
- Closing tax evasion loopholes

The act simplified the income tax code by reducing the taxes on ordinary income while raising the taxes on long-term capital gains. The act reduced the top marginal tax rate from 50% to 28%, leading to a higher labor supply available in the economy. Moreover, it reduced government costs and unnecessary expenses and made tax collection effective, financing public goods and services.

The Taxpayer Relief Act (1997)

This act brought about major and positive changes to the tax code. Taxpayers now receive several tax reduction opportunities, such as education credits and relief for owners selling their houses.

Some of the advantages are:

- Lifetime learning tax credit
- Student loan interest deductibility
- Education IRAs

Because of this act, the top marginal long-term capital gains rate fell from 28% to 20%, and retirement accounts were exempted from capital gains taxes.

The Trademark Act (1946)

This act governs trademarks and their registration and provides causes and actions that protect trademark rights from infringement. It protects the trademark owner by preventing others from using a trademark without permission or in a confusing manner.

Under this law, the term "trademark" includes any trademark, collective mark, service mark or certification mark.

The Unemployment Compensation Amendments (UCA)

In 1992, the Emergency Unemployment Compensation Act of 1991 was amended, which increased the weeks of federally funded unemployment benefits payable for weeks of unemployment.

This amendment allows employees who lose their jobs to roll over their employer-sponsored retirement savings into a qualified retirement plan, such as an IRA, without any tax payment. Employees are given the option of direct transfer to the new account, which is not considered taxable income.

The Uniformed Services Employment and Reemployment Rights Act (1994)

USERRA is a federal law that protects service members' and veterans' civilian employment rights. It requires employers to put individuals back to work and protect them from discrimination in the workplace based on affiliation.

The law minimizes the disadvantages to an individual when that person needs to be absent from civilian employment to serve in the uniformed forces. It does not apply to guard members on active state duty, self-employed individuals, partners or students.

The Workforce Innovation and Opportunity Act (2014)

This act reaffirms the ongoing role of American job centers. Its purpose is to:

- Promote program coordination, key employment, education and training programs at all levels
- Build on previously proven sector strategies, career pathways and work-based training
- Complement and support the job-driven workforce motto
- Improve services to disabled individuals
- Enhance workforce services for the unemployed

The Walsh-Healey Act (1936)

The act establishes minimum standards for work on federal contracts. It requires that all contracts with any part of the government for goods or supplies worth at least $10,000 must:

- Have the name of the supplier as a manufacturer or regular dealer in supplies
- Require no more than eight hours of work a day or forty hours a week
- Have no employees under eighteen
- Require no work to be done under hazardous or unsanitary circumstances

Laws for 15 or More Employees

The Americans with Disability Act (ADA)

The act prohibits discrimination against individuals with disabilities in all areas of life, whether the public or the workplace, schools, transportation, etc.

The Equal Employment Opportunity Act (EEOA) 1972

This act enforced the Civil Rights Act of 1964. It also expanded the scope of civil rights protection to state and local government employees.

The EEOA ensures no discrimination or harassment in the workplace.

The Genetic Information Nondiscrimination Act (GINA) 2008

According to GINA, an employer cannot unlawfully share genetic information regarding an employee with another employee.

The law prohibits employers from inquiring about genetic test results or an employee's or their family's medical history. It protects employees without a manifested condition.

Guidelines on Discrimination Because of Sex (1980)

Under this act, everyone is protected from sexual discrimination. Sexual harassment in the workplace is a violation of the law and unwelcome conduct of a sexual nature constitutes sexual harassment.

Under these conditions, an employer can be liable for sexual discrimination against an employee.

The Pregnancy Discrimination Act (1978)

This law prohibits discrimination based on pregnancy, childbirth or medical conditions related to pregnancy in employment. It requires employers and coworkers to treat pregnant women no differently from other employees.

The Uniform Guidelines on Employee Selection Procedures (1978)

These guidelines were issued to help employers make employment decisions with equity, such as hiring, selection and retention. They provide employers guidance on determining if their selection procedures are according to Title VII.

A selection procedure that harms the hiring, promotion or other opportunities of members of any race, sex or ethnic group is considered discriminatory and inconsistent with these guidelines.

Laws for 20 or More Employees

The Age Discrimination in Employment Act (ADEA) 1967

This law states that it's unlawful for an employer to:

- Refuse or fail to hire or discharge individuals or discriminate against them concerning their compensation, terms, conditions or privileges of employment due to the person's age.
- Limit or segregate employees in any way which would deprive them of employment opportunities because of age.
- Reduce the wage rate.

The Older Workers Benefit Protection Act (1990)

OWBPA requires employers to offer those 40 or older benefits equal to those provided to younger workers.

It also prohibits age-based discrimination in early retirement and other benefit plans by strictly imposing guidelines on employers requiring their employees to sign release forms waiving their rights.

Laws for 50 or More Employees

Executive Order 11246: Affirmative Action (1965)

Under this law, all government contractors and subcontractors are required to take affirmative action to expand job opportunities for minorities. The law established the Office of Federal Contract Compliance (OFCC) in the Department of Labor. It requires that applicants not be subjected to discrimination due to race, sex, religion and other factors.

The Family and Medical Leave Act (1993)

Under this act, an employee can take leave from work for 12 weeks within the year without losing his or her job. The leave will be unpaid, but the employee will maintain his or her pre-existing health benefits.

The leave can be taken due to illness, to care for a newborn or to attend to obligatory family affairs.

Executive Order 13706

This order applies to contractors and subcontractors. It provides that for every 30 hours of work, an employee is allowed to take one hour off with payment.

The law applies to contracts made after 2017 and all direct or indirect employees. It allows employees to take paid sick leave in case of physical or mental illness, visit a health provider or care for a child or spouse.

Laws for 100 or More Employees

The Worker Adjustment and Retraining Notification Act (1988)

The act, passed in 1988, aims to safeguard workers and their communities by mandating that employers give 60-day notice prior to covered plant closings and mass layoffs.

Employers must provide this notice to the affected workers or their representatives, such as labor unions, state-dislocated worker units and the relevant local government unit.

Moreover, the act covers employment losses, such as terminations, layoffs that extend beyond six months, and reductions of more than 50% of employees' work hours in any six-month period.

Laws for Federal Government Employees

The Privacy Act (1974)

The act established a code of fair information practice that governs the collection, maintenance, use and dissemination of personal information maintained in federal agencies' records.

The Patriot Act (2001)

This act allows investigators to gather information when looking into chemical weapons offenses, the use of weapons of mass destruction and terrorism financing.

Under this law, the FBI can secretly conduct a physical search or wiretap an American citizen for evidence of a crime without proving probable cause. Law enforcement agencies can also search phones and emails and gather medical or financial records more quickly under this act.

Moreover, immigration authorities can detain and deport immigrants suspected of terrorism.

Foreign National Visas

There are several types of foreign national visas. Some include:

E Non-immigrant Visas

Non-immigrant visas under category E are reserved for treaty traders (E-1) or treaty investors (E-2). Individuals holding these visas can legally reside in the US and manage the trade or investments of a US business or provide essential skills to the enterprise. Once their E status is terminated, they must leave the US.

Dependents, including spouses and children (under 21) of treaty traders, treaty investors or employees of enterprises, can also obtain a dependent E visa. However, they must not share the same nationality as the applicant.

H Visas

A non-immigrant visa allows employers to petition for highly qualified foreign individuals to work in specialty occupations. A bachelor's degree or higher in a field is required for a position to qualify for H1B status.

H1-B1 visa applicants must demonstrate that they will be residing in the US temporarily and do not intend to immigrate to the country.

In contrast, H1B visa applicants have plans to immigrate to the US. They can also apply for permanent residence.

L-1 Intracompany Transferee

The L-1 visa enables a US employer to transfer a manager or executive from an affiliated foreign office to one of its offices in the US. L-1 employees cannot change or shift companies while they hold this visa.

L-1 can be only filed by the parent or subsidiary branch of the company where the employee has worked for at least a year as a manager, executive or specialized knowledge worker.

O-1 Alien of Extraordinary Ability Visa

O-1 is a non-immigrant visa for an individual with extraordinary science, arts, education, business and athletics ability. It has two types:

O-1A Beneficiary: Someone who has sustained national or international acclaim and is at the top of their field.

O-1B (Arts) Beneficiary: Someone who has gotten national or international acclaim and achieved distinctions in the arts field.

P Visa Categories

The P visa allows foreign nationals who are athletes, artists and entertainers to enter the US for a specific event, competition or performance. A P1 visa is for athletes and their coaches or support staff, and a P2 visa is for artists and entertainers.

EB Employment Visas

An EB visa is employment-based. The preferred immigrant categories include priority workers, aliens with extraordinary abilities in science or arts and outstanding professors and researchers.

Several types of EB visa categories are:

- EB-1: Professors
- EB-2: Lawyers or doctors
- EB-3: Teachers and engineers
- EB-4: Special immigrants
- EB-5: Immigrant investors

Chapter 13: Labor Relations and Collective Bargaining

Relationships between employers and employees are of the utmost importance when it comes to the general functioning of the organization. Labor relations generally focus on fostering healthy work environments, ensuring fair pay and developing a sense of trust between the two parties.

Collective bargaining refers to the processes involving a union representative and the higher-ups in the organization. The negotiation process between employers and a group of employees aims to determine the conditions of employment.

In this chapter, we'll discuss the history behind labor movements, the concept of collective bargaining, how it came to be, the role of unions and the impact of labor laws on collective bargaining.

What is the Labor Movement?

The labor movement was started by workers to fight for their rights to be treated fairly and justly. US laborers once had little to no say in how they were treated, the most problematic issue being that they felt that they had no choice but to work in adverse work environments with little pay.

The labor movement was of paramount importance to the entire labor market, as it ensured that workers were not subject to exploitation. To achieve this, the laborers took action to voice their issues by selecting a representative from among them to negotiate new work terms that safeguarded their rights.

This mass movement is now protected by the government as a federal law. It empowers workers to voice their concerns about their right to healthy work environments and stable work conditions.

The Link Between Employee Engagement and Unionization

Unionization and employee engagement are two crucial concepts researched in depth in the corporate sector. The former means organizing or joining a labor union, whereas employee engagement measures how dedicated and engaged a person is to his or her job.

Employee engagement and unionization have a complicated relationship. On one hand, unionization may boost worker participation by giving employees a voice in joint negotiations for improved pay, benefits and workplace conditions.

On the other hand, unionization may lead to lower employee participation if the union does not reflect the interests of the employees or if there is a breakdown in communication between the union and the employer.

It is essential to see employee engagement and unionization as interrelated. However, their functioning is not dependent on the other.

Employers must note that by pushing for a positive relationship between them and the unions or the employees in general, they can create pleasant work environments where the rights and interests of the employees are protected and also boost the company's productivity in the long run.

What Do Unions Want?

The goals of unions include upholding the rights of their members, securing equitable pay and benefits and enhancing working conditions. Moreover, unions push for greater worker protection laws, rules and policies.

Unions ensure that employees are treated with respect and dignity, receive fair compensation for their job and sufficient benefits, and foster cooperation and respect between employers and workers.

Unions also ensure security in the form of these arrangements:

Closed Shop

An arrangement for union security known as a "closed shop" is between an employer and a labor union.

It mandates work at a specific location of the business. All employees must be union members. This implies the union can only accept members who work at that specific workplace and the company can only hire union members.

A closed-shop arrangement is frequently utilized to protect the jobs of union members and ensure that the union can continue to bargain effectively.

Union Shop

In a union shop, workers must be a part of the unions representing them while also paying their dues. By doing this, the union can ensure that everyone in the bargaining unit is paying their dues and that everyone's interests are represented.

Agency Shop

An agency shop is different from a union shop because non-union members must pay union dues; however, there is no requirement to join. This ensures a fair monetary contribution for non-union members while also reaping the benefits from union activities.

Maintenance of Membership Arrangement

The maintenance of the membership arrangement approach aims to safeguard the union's negotiating strength and guarantee that all workers get the same compensation and benefits.

The union and the employer may benefit from maintaining membership agreements since it ensures that the union can represent the interests of all employees and that the firm can keep a steady workforce.

Unions and the Law

Unions are regulated and formed under strict laws that govern labor relations. Federal and state laws safeguard the rights of union members, employers and the general public.

These laws support the establishment of unions, the negotiating of collective bargaining agreements and the enforcement of labor contracts. They also provide for mediating labor problems or other methods of resolving them.

The following are laws involved in shaping the relationships between unions and employers.

The Norris-LaGuardia Act (1932)

A federal law known as the Norris-LaGuardia Act, passed in 1932, forbade employers from using restrictive measures to prevent employees from joining labor unions.

It restricted the ability of federal courts to grant injunctions against labor disputes and prevented businesses from discriminating against workers based on their participation in or membership in unions.

The act prohibited businesses from making employees sign agreements that would give up their right to form a union. As it gave them more protection and legal options in the case of employment discrimination or unfair labor practices, this act was a significant triumph for labor unions and employees.

The National Labor Relations Act (1935)

This act was discussed earlier in the book, but bears repeating. An important law, the NLRA of 1935 guaranteed workers' rights to participate in collective bargaining with employers. Additionally, it created the NLRB to track and defend these rights.

Workers obtained the ability to form associations and participate in collective bargaining because of the NLRA.

This particular legislation was a substantial victory for employees and represented an important turning point in the labor movement in the United States.

The Taft-Hartley Act (1947)

This law limited unions' authority, especially in terms of organizing and striking, and revised the NLRA.

The Taft-Hartley Act also allowed states to enact right-to-work legislation, which forbade unions from requiring their members to pay dues to work.

The Union Drive and Election

The process of opting to be represented, then selecting a union representative is known as the union drive and election. The process reflects a straightforward electoral approach involving campaigns, community outreach and election.

Let's take a quick look at how it all works.

Initial Contact

At this stage, unions reach out to employees who may have shown some interest in representing their needs. This involves meetings with potential representatives.

Obtaining Authorization Cards

Once representatives have been scouted, the union requests employees sign an authorization card to show that they have selected the individual to represent them. This is important for the electoral procedures to begin.

Holding a Hearing

The NLRB must hold a hearing to evaluate whether a representative election must be held or not. Any opposition to the elections is considered during these hearings.

Engaging in the Campaign

Once the NLRB has determined the need for an election, the campaign process may begin.

At this stage, the union and employer must both be involved in informational activities regarding the need for union representation so that the employees can make an informed decision.

Holding the Election

The elections are held where the eligible voters can cast votes for whom they would like to represent them. Elections are based on majority votes.

What is Collective Bargaining?

Worker and employer representatives determine the terms and conditions of employment via the collective bargaining process, which addresses pay, work schedules, benefits, working environment and other employment-related issues.

A third-party negotiator, such as a union representative, usually facilitates this process by mediating between the parties. Employees may influence choices that impact their working conditions and argue for higher pay and benefits through collective bargaining.

Collective bargaining aims to reach a mutually advantageous agreement between the employer and the employees.

What is Good Faith?

The concept of good faith involves an honest and empathetic approach to collective bargaining procedures. Both parties are expected to act transparently and remain committed to their duties.

The approach requires that both parties proceed with the negotiations in a manner where cooperation and communication are key, building positivity between both parties.

Bargaining Guidelines

For successful bargaining/negotiations, some of the following points must be kept in mind while approaching the process:

- Being courteous and competent.
- Being solution focused.
- Placing a priority on shared interests.
- Refraining from utilizing forceful methods.

The focus should be for both parties to attempt to meet each other halfway, providing room for benefit for both sides.

Impasses, Mediation and Strikes

Impasses are situations where negotiations reach a point where the bargaining process is going nowhere and neither of the parties can come to an agreement or a compromise.

When this happens, mediation is held to break the deadlock and encourage a mutually beneficial agreement for both parties. However, there are also cases where mediation may be of no help.

The union may choose to hold strikes when no other options exist. Strikes, however, risk becoming aggressive, so employers and unions try their best to take up good-faith approaches to keep the lines of negotiations open.

Strike Guidelines

Strikes involve the withdrawal of workers from the workplace until the respective demands are met.

Due to the aggressive nature of strikes, a guideline has been developed to make sure that the strikes do not develop into violent outbursts and follow a certain code of conduct to protect employees and public safety.

The guidelines include:

Peaceful Protests

Employees can engage in peaceful protests and demonstrations close to or outside the workplace.

Non-Aggressive Approach

Keeping in line with the peaceful approach, a non-aggressive approach must be used while protesting. This means there is no room for using force or violent measures.

Protect Property

Property belonging to the organization or the public must not be harmed. This includes public spaces or routes.

Refrain From Harassing Others

Workers on strike must refrain from harassing or threatening replacement workers or those who refuse to take part in the strike.

Comply with Labor Laws

Compliance with labor laws for union members and employers is paramount.

The Contract Agreement

The contract agreement is a legally binding document between an employer and a union that outlines the terms and conditions of employment for unionized employees.

It covers wages, hours, benefits, working conditions, job security and dispute resolution procedures. The agreement is typically negotiated between the union and the employer through collective bargaining. It's subject to federal and state labor laws.

The contract agreement is usually in effect for a set period, usually two or three years, and is renegotiated at the end of the term. It is important for both the employer and the union to adhere to the terms of the agreement and follow the procedures outlined in the contract to resolve any disputes that may arise.

Handling Disputes and Grievances

Grievances are complaints raised by employees about their working conditions, pay or other work-related issues. They can arise from various sources, including:

- Misunderstandings regarding contract agreements
- Situations where agreements are infringed upon
- Discomfort or disruption in workplace conditions
- Low wages
- Unsafe working conditions
- Unfair treatment
- Discrimination
- Unreasonable workloads
- Unclear job expectations
- Unstable job security
- Unreasonable hours

The Grievance Procedure

This involves the process by which employees can voice their concerns systematically and professionally. It includes the following steps:

- Collecting pertinent details and data relevant to the complaint.
- Filing the grievance to the relevant supervisor or manager.
- Following up with management to confirm the complaint is being handled.
- Raising the complaint to a higher management level (if necessary).
- Considering filing an official complaint or lawsuit if the issue remains unresolved.

Guidelines for Handling Grievances

In order for the grievance process to work, there are several guidelines that both workers and employers must adhere to. These consist of:

- Remaining professional and respectful in all communications.
- Thoroughly recording the stages of the process.
- Ensuring choices are based upon the information on the situation and the collective bargaining agreement conditions.

How to Handle a Grievance Situation

Handling a grievance can be tough. It's essential that a professional with no prejudice address such sensitive topics.

Listed below are a few of the methods to properly deal with grievances.

Make the Employee Feel Heard

Place yourself in the employee's position and look at things from the person's perspective. Actively listen to the expressed concerns and gather relevant information to help you better understand the situation.

Conduct an Investigation

A thorough and detailed investigation is vital to find a fair solution to the grievance. It is important to collect unbiased, factual information.

Follow Protocol

Companies usually have procedures set in place for unfortunate situations that require filing grievances. It is important to follow the guidelines prepared by the company to ensure fair handling of the situation.

Remove Bias and Be Transparent

It is important to remain neutral and transparent throughout the procedure and avoid siding with either party.

Come to a Solution

The ultimate goal is to resolve the grievance in a way that is fair to all parties involved. This may involve reaching an agreement or taking disciplinary action if necessary.

Chapter 14: Risk Assessment Techniques for a Safe Workplace

Developing a secure workplace is the main priority for a company. In order to obtain this, it is important to have a thorough understanding and knowledge of the workplace. Risk analysis is a systematic method of assessing possible risks.

Why is Safety Important?

A secure place of work is crucial not just for workers' well-being but for a company's success. It protects workers from bodily injury and harm, positively affecting retention, productivity and employee morale.

In addition, a healthy and safe atmosphere can improve employee satisfaction and reduce turnover rates. An organization with a track record of developing a secure work environment will have a good image and can draw in top talent.

Therefore, applying good safety measures and strategies is a wise action to take. This type of thinking benefits businesses in the long term.

Advantages of a Secure Workplace

- A healthy workplace possesses numerous advantages for both workers and employers. A few of these include:
- It may lead to fewer injuries or accidents at the office.
- This raises the workers' motivation and results in better productivity and efficiency.
- It creates trust between personnel and supervisors, boosting retention.
- It enables workers to concentrate on their job, leading to reduced turnover and absenteeism rates.

Companies additionally reap the benefits of a secure work environment, such as:

- Decreased workers' compensation costs.

- Positive business reputation and public perception.
- Better employee quality.

Companies are legally responsible for developing a secure working environment for their personnel. Failing to offer a safe work atmosphere could incur legal action and penalties.

Top Management's Role in Safety

The support and commitment of senior management are important to make sure that security is a high priority at all levels of the business. Management is accountable for supplying a secure environment for staff members.

1. It's accountable for developing and implementing a safety philosophy in the company. This entails developing policies and implementing methods that encourage safety and dealing with possible hazards.

2. It ensures staff members are appropriately trained to understand and react to possible risks.

3. It routinely evaluates the company's security plan's effectiveness.

The Supervisor's Role in Accident Prevention

Supervisors play an important part in accident avoidance at work. They're responsible for:

- Being knowledgeable about safety procedures.
- Monitoring personnel to make sure they perform correctly and stick to established security guidelines.
- Motivating personnel to report safety issues or dangers they come across. This is often an important aid in avoiding work injuries.
- Keeping a log of incidents to study them and avoid similar incidents.

Occupational Safety Law

OSHA sets and enforces workplace safety standards. Employers are required to comply with OSHA standards to ensure a safe and healthy workplace.

OSHA standards require business owners to keep records of work-related injuries and illnesses and report severe injuries and fatalities to OSHA within 90 days.

Employers must also post OSHA injury and illness summary forms in a prominent location in the workplace.

Inspections and Citations

OSHA conducts inspections of workplaces to ensure employers comply with safety standards. Inspection is prioritized based on a high rate of work-related injuries and illnesses.

The inspection process typically begins with an initial contact with the employer, followed by an opening conference and a walk-around inspection of the workplace. During the inspection, OSHA inspectors will identify any hazards or violations of safety standards.

Employers who fail to comply with OSHA standards may face fines and citations. OSHA also has the authority to issue stop-work orders to prevent work from continuing until safety violations are corrected.

OSHA has an annual record of the violations cited within the country; for example, the most cited OSHA violation of 2019 was fall protection. Six thousand and ten violations were recorded.

Rights and Responsibilities of Employers and Employees Under OSHA

Employers must create a secure and healthy workplace complying with OSHA standards and provide training and education to their employees on safety protocols.

Employees must comply with safety protocols and report safety concerns to their supervisors.

What Causes Accidents?

Accidents at the office may be a result of several factors, including:

Insufficiently Guarded Equipment

This is gear with insufficient security guards or barriers available to safeguard employees from moving parts, sharp edges or several other threats.

An employee could be hurt by a conveyor belt lacking adequate protection, for example.

Defective Equipment

Equipment that is defective could be a big danger. It may explode, for example, resulting in significant injuries or deaths.

Hazardous Procedures Around Machines

Workers improperly trained in the use of certain machinery may be at risk of accidents due to unsafe practices or procedures.

For example, a worker who removes a safety guard to clean a machine may be at risk of injury if the machine is accidentally activated.

Unsafe Storage

Poorly stored materials can pose a significant hazard to workers. For instance, overstacking unstable pallets or items stored in an unsafe location can lead to falls or other accidents.

The improper storage of chemicals can be dangerous because they may cause explosions.

Improper Illumination

Inadequate lighting can create hazards for workers, particularly when visual acuity is important.

Poor lighting can lead to accidents like falls or collisions, and workers may miss warning signs or improperly identify hazards.

Spills

Liquids, powders or other substances spilled on floors can create a slipping hazard, potentially leading to falls or other injuries. Some spilled chemicals, when exposed to the air, may cause reactions.

Tripping Hazards

Workers risk tripping over items left in walkways, poorly maintained flooring or stairs. This can lead to sprains, broken bones or other injuries.

The area should be kept clean and tidy for the employees to move freely and perform their jobs without worrying about their safety.

Working From Heights

Workers who perform tasks from high positions may be at risk of falls, particularly if they don't have appropriate fall protection equipment or are not properly trained in safe practices.

Electrical Hazards

Electrical accidents can occur if workers come into contact with live wires or improperly grounded equipment. These accidents can cause electrical burns, shocks or electrocution, which may lead to coma or death.

How to Limit Workplace Accidents

There are several ways to limit or control accidents in the workplace. These include:

Reducing Unsafe Conditions

Employers can take several steps to reduce unsafe conditions in the workplace, including proper maintenance of equipment and machinery and providing proper training to employees on how to operate equipment safely.

Safety protocols should be printed and openly displayed so the workers may understand. For example, posters on handwashing were displayed during the COVID-19 pandemic.

Workers should also be given training in case of an accident, so they may be able to cope during an emergency.

Ensuring the workplace is properly ventilated and illuminated and that employees have clear pathways to move around the workspace can also help reduce accidents.

Conducting Operational Safety Reviews

Regular safety reviews can help identify potential hazards and unsafe conditions in the workplace.

A review can be conducted by a safety professional or an internal safety committee made up of employees with the expertise to identify potential hazards. It should examine all workplace areas, including production areas, storage and offices.

The findings should be documented so they can help reduce future crises.

Using Personal Protective Equipment (PPE)

Employers can give employees access to personal protective equipment (PPE), such as hard hats, gloves, safety glasses and earplugs, to reduce accidents. They should properly train employees on using and caring for PPE. Moreover, they should ensure that PPE fits properly and is appropriate for the job.

How to Reduce Unsafe Acts

Business owners can encourage and facilitate safe workplace behavior by following these steps:

Screening

Employers can help reduce harmful incidents in the workplace by screening employees for their physical ability to perform job duties and their knowledge and experience regarding their designated job.

This can help to ensure employees are better equipped to handle the demands of their job and are less likely to engage in unsafe behavior.

Training

Providing comprehensive hands-on training to employees can help reduce unsafe acts by ensuring they have a thorough understanding of their job duties and the safety procedures and equipment necessary to perform those duties safely.

Regular training can also help to reinforce safe behavior and ensure that employees are up to date on the latest safety protocols.

Promoting a Culture of Safety

Creating a culture of security at the office will be the main job of the employer, a setting where workers realize the benefits of security and feel inspired to take measures to defend themselves and their colleagues.

Developing a Supportive Environment

Employers have the capability to lessen unsafe actions in the office by developing a supportive atmosphere where people feel at ease reporting incidents or safety concerns. This ensures safety issues are resolved promptly.

Creating a Safety Policy

A definite security policy outlines the organization's resolve for safety and the precise protocols necessary to keep a safe environment. This safety policy must be followed consistently by the employees.

Behavior-based Safety and Safety Awareness Programs

Behavior-based security is a method that informs the employees and the management of the general security of your office through safety observations.

Safety awareness programs help instruct workers on safe behavior and encourage them to avoid injuries and accidents.

Worker Participation

Employers can steadily reduce the number of unsafe acts by involving workers, soliciting feedback on security procedures and encouraging them to report incidents or safety concerns. Personnel also can share their ideas about the upkeep of workplace safety.

Workplace Health Hazards: Problems and Solutions

There are numerous hazards employees can encounter in their workplaces.

Chemical and Industrial Hygiene

Workplace chemical hazards can result in major health issues, including breathing problems, skin irritation, organ damage and cancer.

Workers subjected to harsh chemicals should be supplied with protection like respirators and appropriate clothing, along with proper ventilation. Workers must be properly informed about the chemicals they're handling and their harmful effects.

Companies should avoid chemical spills, leaks and other incidents that can expose workers to dangerous materials. Crisis management teams must be prepared in case of an accident.

Alcoholism and Substance Abuse

Substance abuse and addiction can greatly impact workplace safety, efficiency and worker wellness.

Companies are able to help stop substance abuse by providing employee assistance programs, providing training and education on substance abuse and implementing drug testing policies.

A simple security check of individuals as they enter the office will make certain that there are no drugs in the vicinity.

Stress, Burnout and Depression

Workplace stress can result in depression and burnout, adversely affecting employee well-being, productivity and security.

Companies can lessen stress by promoting work-life balance, offering resources and support for brain well-being and producing a good work environment.

Outdoor activities or team-building exercises provide stress relief from the daily grind of work.

Solving Computer-Related Ergonomic Problems

Prolonged computer use can cause ergonomic problems such as eye strain, carpal tunnel syndrome and neck and back pain.

Employers can reduce the risk of ergonomic problems by providing ergonomic workstations, such as adjustable chairs, keyboards and monitors.

Employee comfort should be a concern for the employer as this is directly related to productivity or output. This also affects the company's reputation and long-term goals.

Repetitive Motion Disorders

Repetitive motion disorders can result from repeatedly performing the same physical task, such as using a computer mouse or typing.

Employers can reduce the risk of repetitive motion disorders by providing ergonomic workstations, limiting the time employees spend performing repetitive tasks and providing regular breaks.

This can also be avoided if the work schedule is more flexible and employee comfort is considered crucial.

Sitting

Prolonged sitting can lead to health problems such as back pain, obesity and cardiovascular disease.

Employers can promote employee health by encouraging frequent breaks and providing standing workstations. Health-related seminars can be conducted, which can make the workers concerned for their health and lead to exercise or a healthy lifestyle.

Infectious Diseases

Workplace exposure to infectious diseases can lead to serious health problems. Employers can help prevent the spread of infectious diseases by promoting good hygiene, providing hand sanitizer and other hygiene products and promoting vaccination.

Restrooms should be cleaned frequently throughout the day and soap should be provided for handwashing. An overall hygienic environment should be encouraged. Waste baskets should be emptied daily and color-coded bins should be used for hazardous or toxic materials.

Workplace Smoking

Smoking at the office can result in breathing issues and other health problems. Businesses can promote worker health by offering smoke-free environments, implementing smoking cessation programs and advocating healthy lifestyle choices.

How to Secure the Workplace

Installation safeguards are crucial to workplace security. This involves evaluating risks and installing organizational, natural and mechanical security solutions to guard against possible threats.

The procedure calls for several actions, such as:

Analyzing the Threat Risk

Evaluate the present threat. This may be achieved via a threat analysis, which considers elements including the kind of business, the place and the criminal activity in the region.

Putting in Place Mechanical, Natural and Organizational Security Systems

Once the risk has been assessed, setting up the proper security measures is essential.

Mechanical security measures may consist of locks, security systems and cameras, whereas all-natural security systems incorporate obstacles like fencing, bollards and organic components like bushes and trees.

Organizational security solutions may incorporate protocols, policies and methods dealing with potential security risks.

A security guard should be equipped with a firearm in the event of a major threat. Security systems must be furnished with devices that alert the police immediately in case of a possible risk.

Regularly Reviewing Potential Threats

It is essential to regularly look at possible threats and upgrade security plans. This may be achieved via frequent risk assessments as well as security inspections.

How to Protect Workers from Terrorist Attacks

Protecting workers from terrorist acts entails taking measures to reduce the danger of an assault and establishing a strategy to react in the face of an assault. Some crucial measures to safeguard personnel from terrorist acts consist of:

Carrying Out a Risk Assessment: This entails evaluating the possibility of a terrorist attack and its possible effect on your personnel and company.

Creating an Emergency Response Plan: This should incorporate specific methods for how to proceed in case of a terrorist attack, such as evacuation procedures, communication procedures and designated meeting points.

Give Employees Training: Employees should be provided directions on how to proceed in the event of a terrorist attack, such as the proper way to report suspicious behavior.

Apply Physical Security Measures: This could consist of installing security cameras, access control techniques and extra measures to restrict access to your premises.

Keep Open Lines of Communication: Employees must be motivated to report suspicious activities.

Stay Informed: Keep updated with the most recent threat information and modify your security measures if needed.

The Significance of Cybersecurity: Cybersecurity protects computers, networks and critical data from stealing, damage and unauthorized access. It is crucial for safeguarding sensitive information, preserving security and protecting a company's reputation.

Cybersecurity includes:

- Using strong passwords.
- Encrypting sensitive data.
- Setting up firewalls and antivirus programs.
- Regularly upgrading software programs and security patches.

Employers should also obtain cybersecurity instruction to avoid the spread of viruses.

Cyberattacks can happen to anybody and may lead to economic losses, loss of client trust and bankruptcy.

People may also be victims of cybercrime, like online scams, cyberbullying and identity theft. Thus, companies, individuals and governments must safeguard their sensitive networks and systems data.

Chapter 15: Organizational Restructuring Initiatives: Risk to Business Continuity

Organizational change refers to a company's actions to alter its fundamental elements, including its practices, culture, workforce, offerings, infrastructure and technological advancements.

Managers are typically tasked with implementing organizational change initiatives once chosen. A change management strategy helps managers avoid unfavorable consequences like business interruption, lost productivity and revenues and closure. It can ensure business continuity.

What is Business Continuity Management?

Business continuity management (BCM) refers to the proactive planning and preparation done to guarantee that an organization can carry out its essential business tasks in the event of an emergency.

An emergency can include pandemics, corporate crises, natural catastrophes, workplace violence or any other occurrence that prevents an organization from operating normally.

Effective Business Continuity Plans

An effective business continuity plan will use change management strategies to ensure the company promotes a culture where all employees are sufficiently aware of everyday hazards and their individual responsibilities to report, manage and mitigate risks.

Consider a finance firm with headquarters in a major city. It may put a business continuity plan in place by backing up its systems and client files elsewhere. As a result, the company's satellite offices can continue to access crucial information if something happens to the primary office.

HR's Role in Ensuring Business Continuity

HR managers have a special responsibility when it comes to business continuity planning. They provide information and analysis on the most crucial aspect of every organization: its workforce. This makes HR a crucial participant and resource in sustaining or resuming business operations following a significant event.

HR is responsible for:

- Creating and putting into practice business continuity strategies.
- Figuring out which operations are essential to the company, which must continue to operate in an emergency.
- Providing guidelines and practices for workers' behavior when a disturbance occurs.
- Giving employees disaster preparedness training.
- Ensuring companies continue operating even in challenging situations.

Role of HR in Major Business Changes

In case of huge changes like a corporate merger, acquisition or integration, some unique business continuity risks and opportunities need to be addressed. Not surprisingly, all these changes require HR to play an active role.

Mergers and Acquisitions

With companies like Amazon and Google generating news for their significant commercial transactions, mergers and acquisitions are currently all the rage. Global merger and acquisition activity reached $5.9 trillion in 2021, a 64% rise from 2020.

Most acquisitions involve technology, finance, industrials, energy and power. But why are mergers and acquisitions so successful despite the risks they come with? After all, they require large-scale organizational change.

A successful merger or acquisition depends on several intricate moving parts, but one crucial component is prompt and secure data integration. An "underestimation of IT problems" was reported as the cause of merger and acquisition failure by 34% of financial services organizations in 2016.

Data aggregation, integrating data warehouses and other data sets, and implementing new tools and applications to process the data are some examples of IT solutions that can be combined.

Take the example of a famous acquisition: Disney, Pixar and Marvel. Walt Disney Co. paid $7.4 billion to acquire Pixar in 2006, and the company has since seen great success with movies like *WALL-E, Finding Dory* and *Toy Story 3*, each of which has brought in billions of dollars for the business.

Integration

Business integration is when a corporation unifies its various technical models to ensure they align and sync with the corporate culture. When this happens, there is no division in and of itself because the data once handled by a single program is now managed by many.

The same is true of functions. These are combined to establish a complete relationship, making it easier to concentrate them into a single shared database type.

Coordinating each company's IT and business integration, by definition, fosters communication flow. This, in turn, encourages the business culture and goals to integrate technology.

Relectric is a company that has undergone successful integration. It is a renowned provider of electrical components with same-day shipment available on more than one million parts from 22 domestic sites.

Relectric implemented an ERP, shipping and CRM connectivity solution to simplify identifying parts and letting customers know about shipping status. The components were placed into Relectric's CRM system as metadata and then synced up with the website database every 30 minutes. This made it much simpler to decide which parts needed to be ordered again, where they should be shipped from, etc.

Offshoring

When a business offshores, it transfers some of its operations from its home country to a different one to take advantage of lower costs.

A company that struggles to find qualified employees in its local market can consider offshoring. With this engagement model, the company can offer the product or service and save money.

Moreover, offshoring can allow a company to receive top-notch development, scale its business, reach overseas markets and allocate expenditures more effectively.

Downsizing

Downsizing lowers operating expenses and makes a company leaner. It entails lowering the number of employees, closing plants and improving the productivity and efficiency of the company's departments.

The goal of downsizing is to restructure a corporation to increase its competitiveness. It is a logical step in an organization's evolution; however, downsizing is challenging for a company like any other change.

Employee morale might be negatively impacted by downsizing. And as the workplace changes, innovation declines and voluntary turnover rates may rise over time.

To overcome these consequences, HR must reassure the remaining staff members about the issue and keep them updated. It should make sure that employees are aware of the challenges and describe why restructuring and downsizing are crucial.

Test 1: Questions

(1) HR management is the process of __________.

(A) Workforce building, problem solving, policy making

(B) Hiring, organizing and managing the workforce

(C) Working with customers, performing talent acquisition, advertising and employees

(D) None of the above

(2) What are the two responsibilities of an HR department?

(A) Talent acquisition, performance management

(B) Career planning, training

(C) Compliance, dealing with regulations

(D) Publishing for recruitment needs, hiring

(3) The HR department maintains employee relations by _______.

(A) Providing more employee benefits

(B) Developing performance standards and giving feedback

(C) Attracting and recruiting talent

(D) Maintaining a positive work environment

(4) Which of the following are internal factors for firms to manage their staff?

(A) Management style

(B) Competition

(C) Rules and regulations

(D) Technological advancements

(5) Employee demographics influence the __________.

(A) Kinds of benefits employees may want

(B) Type of training a company must provide to its employees

(C) Rules and regulations of a company

(D) Morale of a company

(6) Employee categorization means _________.

(A) An agreement made between employees and managers on objectives that have to be accomplished in a specific time frame

(B) Giving a specific task to several different employees

(C) Dividing employees based on criteria like experiences, abilities and skills

(D) None of the above

(7) Which is not a type of employee classification?

(A) Skilled vs. unskilled

(B) Full time vs. part time

(C) Professional vs. entry-level

(D) Permanent vs. temporary

(8) Which of the following is characteristic of a recruitment/section plan?

(A) It outlines the steps an organization will take to identify, attract and hire new employees.

(B) It outlines the steps an organization will take to retain its employees and prevent high levels of turnover.

(C) It outlines the steps an organization will take to dismiss surplus or redundant employees.

(D) None of the above.

(9) The recruitment/section plan involves _____________.

(A) College recruiting events

(B) In-person interviews

(C) Résumé reviews

(D) Behavioral assessments

(10) Organizations develop and implement a retention plan to lower staff turnover and improve employee engagement.

A retention plan can include information on __________.

(A) Recruitment sources

(B) Work-life balance

(C) Job analysis and description

(D) None of the above

(11) During job analyses, what type of information can you get about jobs?

(A) Duties

(B) Responsibilities

(C) Skills

(D) All of the above

(12) Job analysis information is often utilized in ________.

(A) Providing training and development

(B) Reducing unemployment and turnover

(C) Increasing employee engagement

(D) None of the above

(13) What is a priority when finding market information about jobs?

(A) Finding the purpose of job analysis

(B) Selecting the correct method

(C) Performing data collection

(D) All of the above

(14) A job description refers to __________.

(A) Identifying and attracting employees with the right skills to fill a role within an organization

(B) Making use of simulations, assessments and tests to understand job applicants'/current employees' knowledge, abilities and skills

(C) A written document that outlines the requirements of a job within a company

(D) None of the above

(15) What do interviews help HR understand?

(A) If a candidate is a good fit for the job

(B) What a candidate brings to the position

(C) How a candidate works through problems

(D) All of the above.

(16) __________ can help jumpstart the onboarding process.

(A) Evaluating the cultural fit

(B) Verifying information

(C) Collecting data

(D) None of the above

(17) What is a key consideration when preparing for an interview?

(A) Collecting relevant data

(B) Giving company-specific knowledge

(C) Verifying candidates' information

(D) Defining the requirements of the job

(18) What is/are the primary target(s) of an organization that wants to be the best company to work for?

(A) Trained employees

(B) Increased focus

(C) Market success

(D) Continuous product innovation

(19) What is an activity that focuses on an employee's role or action?

(A) Training

(B) Development

(C) Development of skill sets

(D) Evaluation of performance

(20) What is the purpose of employee orientation?

(A) Introducing the company to new employees

(B) Increasing workforce productivity

(C) Evaluating candidates' performance

(D) All of the above

(21) An organizational learning strategy sets out __________ and __________ for employees.

(A) Specific behavior, attitude changes

(B) Required skills, competencies

(C) Job responsibilities, expectations

(D) Performance evaluation criteria

(22) The components of learning objectives are __________.

(A) Audience, behavior, condition, degree

(B) Skills, competencies, behaviors, attitudes

(C) Time, effort, commitment, motivation

(D) Cognitive, psychomotor, affective, social

(23) Which organizational learning strategy promotes specific skills required for company expansion?

(A) Competitive

(B) Corporate

(C) Business

(D) Functional

(24) What is a key role of HR in training and development?

(A) Identifying new market job trends

(B) Evaluating employee benefits

(C) Helping employees reach organizational goals

(D) None of the above

(25) The goal of the HR department of a company is to __________.

(A) Make sure the organization functions optimally

(B) Keep an eye on recruitment

(C) Give out employee benefits

(D) Take care of every employee

(26) What is the purpose of an organizational development program?

(A) Analyzing the company's strengths and weaknesses

(B) Improving the company's overall performance

(C) Creating short-term solutions

(D) Meeting the individual goals of employees

(27) What is the effective characteristic every organizational development program should have?

(A) Short-sightedness

(B) Comprehensiveness

(C) Versatility

(D) Inflexibility

(28) HR's role in organizational development is __________.

(A) Giving out employee benefits

(B) Performing assessments of candidates

(C) Training the workforce

(D) Collaborating with employees

(29) A candidate assessment is a process that helps HR determine the ________.

(A) Potential of an applicant

(B) Strengths of an organization

(C) Weaknesses of an organization

(D) Performance of an employee

(30) The purpose of managerial on-the-job training and rotation is to provide ________.

(A) Employees with new job opportunities

(B) Managers for leadership positions

(C) Opportunities to reduce employee turnover

(D) Employees with opportunities to increase the efficiency of the organization

(31) What are the benefits of on-the-job training?

(A) Reduced productivity, increased training costs

(B) Reduced employee satisfaction, increased training costs

(C) Customized training, immediate application

(D) Increased employee turnover, reduced training costs

(32) An employer of a big multinational company hires five employees. He decides to pay their salary every month.

Which method of payment is the employer opting for?

(A) Aligning total rewards with strategy

(B) Increments in time

(C) The balance sheet approach

(D) Payments of performance

(33) What are the advantages of performance pay?

(A) It can encourage employees to perform at their highest level.

(B) It can aid in attracting and retaining top talent.

(C) It can help align employee and organizational objectives.

(D) All of the above

(34) The manager at a bank hit his quarterly target. He was given an incentive by the top management.

Which of the following is a typical manager incentive?

(A) Stock options

(B) Free parking at work

(C) Increased vacation time

(D) Bonuses for reaching company-wide targets

(35) A team of HR executives held a meeting where they decided to hire new employees and set their pay rate considering the market-based approach.

What is the market-based approach?

(A) Determining how important a job is for an organization

(B) Choosing a job evaluation committee to make decisions about pay rates

(C) Researching the pay levels of a similar job in the external market

(D) None of the above

(36) A company hasn't been paying employees the minimum wage. Previous employees often report less-than-average pay and negative workplace conditions.

What act is the company not adhering to?

(A) The Fair Labor Standards Act

(B) The Davis-Bacon Act

(C) The Walsh-Healey Public Contracts Act

(D) Title VII of the Civil Rights Act

(37) An organization's _______________________ should not be taken into account when formulating a strategic compensation strategy.

(A) Financial resources

(B) Job duties and responsibilities

(C) Geographic location

(D) Number of employees

(38) A major bank has implemented a profit-sharing program for its customer care staff. The plan offers staff a bonus when customer satisfaction ratings are met or exceeded.

Which of the following is a benefit of this plan?

(A) Increased competition and conflict among team members

(B) Decreased emphasis on quality and client satisfaction

(C) Promotion of teamwork and cooperation

(D) Higher fixed compensation expenses for the business

(39) Monetary rewards fall under __________.

(A) Health insurance

(B) Direct compensation

(C) Vacations

(D) None of the above

(40) A gain-sharing plan is a type of pay-for-performance plan in which ___________ receive ___________________.

(A) Employees, stock options

(B) Employees, a share of the company's profits

(C) Managers, compensation based on their tenure

(D) None of the above

(41) Which of the following is an example of a non-monetary reward given to professional employees?

(A) Piecework pay

(B) Merit pay

(C) Stock options

(D) Recognition awards

(42) Money is what drives people to work. Is this true?

(A) Yes. Money is what motivates people to work.

(B) It doesn't motivate people much.

(C) It motivates some people but not others.

(D) None of the above

(43) Internal equity is a compensation concept referring to __________.

(A) Fairness for a specific skill for a similar job in the external market

(B) The fairness of the process used to decide the benefits package

(C) The equality of rewards within an organization for people in comparable positions

(D) How fair a person's pay is compared to what coworkers get for doing the same or similar work in the same company

(44) Through collective bargaining, unions may significantly influence a company's wage decisions and pay policies by establishing minimum pay scales and other compensation-related rules.

Which of the following acts oversees these activities?

(A) The National Labor Relations Act

(B) The National Labor Rights Act

(C) The National Labor Rules Act

(D) The National Labor Regulations Act

(45) Company XYZ has a young workforce and is a start-up. It is considering offering assistance with student debt repayment to its employees.

What is a potential benefit of a program assisting student loan repayment?

(A) Lower employee satisfaction and retention

(B) Better financial health and happiness at work

(C) Increased focus on short-term financial goals over long-term career development

(D) Decreased competition for top talent

(46) Why is independent contractors' pay higher than those with in-office jobs?

(A) They are responsible for their work-related taxes.

(B) The law requires it.

(C) They do risky jobs.

(D) They don't have a formal written agreement.

(47) How does a SWOT analysis help with strategic planning?

(A) It helps assess internal and external factors that affect a company.

(B) It helps to plan a company's areas of improvement.

(C) It helps the organization seize the best opportunities.

(D) All of the above.

(48) SWOT stands for __________.

(A) Strengths, weaknesses, opportunities and treats

(B) Strengths, weaknesses, obstacles and threats

(C) Strengths, weaknesses, opportunities and threats

(D) Strengths, weaknesses, opportunities and terms

(49) Which of the following steps is included in strategic planning?

(A) Delaying responsibilities

(B) Assessing the current position

(C) Continuously changing the company's vision

(D) Not looking for results

(50) What is the best method for encouraging organizational communication?

(A) Letting team members do their work without interfering

(B) Ignoring team members when they ask for help

(C) Promoting an unpleasant environment

(D) Remaining open to feedback and encouraging team members to participate

(51) Resource imitations are included in a company's _______.

(A) Weaknesses

(B) Opportunities

(C) Strengths

(D) Threats

(52) The SWOT analysis includes all factors that affect a company and may build or break a company's future.

According to the SWOT analysis, threats to a company include ______.

(A) Negative press coverage

(B) Increasing product demands

(C) Tangible assets

(D) Good media coverage

(53) By promoting a communication-friendly environment, a company can ________.

(A) Ensure maximum employee proficiency

(B) Encourage friendship and trust

(C) Reduce employee turnover

(D) All of the above

(54) Which of the following is included in organizational communication?

(A) Vertical communication

(B) Oral communication

(C) Formal communication

(D) All of the above

(55) Grapevine communication occurs through social media and other communication platforms.

Grapevine communication is __________.

(A) Formal

(B) Informal

(C) Internal

(D) External

(56) The manager at a company develops a campaign in which she conducts a one-to-one session with clients, talking about the services her company provides to similar prospects.

What type of communication is the manager using?

(A) Formal

(B) Informal

(C) Internal

(D) External

(57) Which of the following is a type of organizational structure that includes functional and product managers?

(A) Matrix

(B) Flatarchy

(C) Divisional

(D) Functional

(58) A type of organizational structure without any management levels is known as a __________.

(A) Matrix structure

(B) Flatarchy

(C) Divisional structure

(D) Functional structure

(59) A company has an HR department, a finance department, a marketing team and a senior manager supervising all these departments.

The company is using a ___________ structure.

(A) Matrix structure

(B) Flatarchy

(C) Divisional structure

(D) Functional structure

(60) Multiple teams working toward one specific goal in an organization are included in a __________.

(A) Matrix structure

(B) Flatarchy

(C) Divisional structure

(D) Functional structure

(61) In a __________ structure, employees are free to pitch new ideas for the company and its products.

(A) Matrix

(B) Flatarchy

(C) Divisional

(D) Functional

(62) What are the key functions of an HRIS?

(A) Data management

(B) Learning management

(C) Time and attendance

(D) All of the above

(63) What is not a function of HRIS?

(A) Data management

(B) Learning management

(C) Time and attendance

(D) Employee retention

(64) Operational goals focus on day-to-day activities ________.

(A) Of the company

(B) Of the employees

(C) That support tactical goals

(D) All of the above

(65) Organizational goals commonly include _________.

(A) Long-term plans

(B) Short-term plans

(C) Discarded plans

(D) Both (A) and (B)

(66) What are HR policies?

(A) Guidelines for managing employees and internal issues

(B) Steps HR must follow to manage employee relations and administration

(C) Daily activities that HR must accomplish

(D) Short-term plans of a company that aid in promoting its vision

(67) Which of the following best defines HR procedures?

(A) Guidelines for managing employees and internal issues

(B) Steps HR must follow to manage employee relations and administration

(C) Daily activities that HR must accomplish

(D) Short-term plans that promote the company's vision

(68) The treatment of employees is outlined in ____________.

(A) HR policies

(B) HR procedures

(C) HR operations

(D) All of the above

(69) How can an organization increase employee engagement?

(A) Take surveys.

(B) Ask employees to work long hours on projects.

(C) Give recognition to employees who work harder.

(D) Expect employees to adjust and learn according to the changes in the company.

(70) _________ gave physical labor workers the right to be paid according to the prevailing wages on public projects

(A) The Dodd-Frank Wall Street Reform and Consumer Protection Act

(B) The Davis-Bacon Act

(C) The Employee Polygraph Protection Act

(D) The Copeland Act

(71) Despite their union's advice to continue negotiating, a group of employees decides to go on strike without giving proper notice to the union or following the required procedures for calling a strike.

What law protects against this type of protest?

(A) The National Labor Relations Act

(B) The Taft-Hartley Act

(C) The Norris-LaGuardia Act

(D) The Employee Polygraph Protection Act

(72) A company decides that it doesn't need to be inspected this year because it has not received any negative feedback from its employees. It works with harsh toxins and chemicals.

Is the decision correct?

(A) According to OSHA, the company's decision could end up causing issues due to defective equipment.

(B) The decision is correct. If the employees have no issues, there is no need for inspection.

(C) The inspection is needed to fulfill lawfully set formalities, but the decision rules are not necessary.

(D) The decision seems very important as the company has greater expertise on how it functions.

(73) What is the difference between FACT and FRCA?

(A) FACT is a federal law, whereas FRCA is an amendment to consumers' credit-related records

(B) FACT is an amendment to improve accuracy, whereas FRCA is a federal law regulating credit information.

(C) FRCA was passed to abolish wages, and FACT is a federal law regulating credit information.

(D) FRCA is a federal law passed for establishing consumer rights, whereas FACT is an act passed for the fairness of labor without discrimination.

(74) A company that works with medicines and machines to mass produce them is asked to implement safety measures to limit accidents.

Which of the following is not an example of a safety measure implementation?

(A) Including proper manuals for the machines to reduce the risk of getting injured and/or damaging the machine

(B) Writing a review on the potential dangers of taking the medicine

(C) Ensuring that employees wear proper attire and have proper equipment

(D) Making sure the work area is properly illuminated to give employees more visibility

(75) What should a company do to prepare for an emergency?

(A) Propose and create an efficient law that regulates preventive measures against disasters.

(B) Acquire an agreement with the laborers to establish fair bargaining.

(C) Make the employees sign a contract not allowing them to leave.

(D) Discuss and create an effective business continuity plan in case of an emergency.

(76) In which of the following cases can the Equal Pay Act (EPA) be implemented?

(A) When a female employee's pay is deducted despite her taking a paid leave due to being pregnant

(B) When a laborer is tasked with working on a fountain for the public park but is not paid due to expenses being over budget

(C) When a consumer's credit card records show an anomaly due to leaked sensitive information

(D) When an employer requests an employee take a private test, interrogating them about private questions irrelevant to the job description, using a lie detector

(77) Which of the following acts mandates a comfortable working environment for people with special needs?

(A) The Rehabilitation Act of 1973

(B) The Occupational Safety and Health Act (OSHA) of 1970

(C) The Service Contract Act of 1965

(D) The Uniformed Services Employment and Reemployment Rights Act of 1994

(78) An employer threatened retaliation, such as firing or demoting union leaders or members, if the union did not accept his proposals.

What is this an example of?

(A) Bad faith bargaining, which uses unfair means

(B) A tactical approach to negotiation

(C) Aggressive tactical bargaining

(D) A productive and fair agreement

(79) What is HR's role in ensuring business continuity?

(A) They provide a workforce analysis of the organization.

(B) They make statistical reports on casualties.

(C) They analyze the emergency's impact on the company.

(D) They are responsible for communication with consumers/customers.

(80) An employee is tasked with typing long articles daily. The company has a policy of paying by productivity hours. As a result, the employee works ten hours every day to make sure he meets his daily target.

What could this issue lead to?

(A) It could lead to the employee being potentially open to incentives.

(B) The employee is likely to have repetitive motion disorder.

(C) The employee could become an alcoholic and a smoker, leading to health issues.

(D) It could result in the employee becoming unhealthy due to an infectious disease.

(81) What is the benefit of integration within a business?

(A) It allows companies to reduce discrimination between genders.

(B) It prevents companies from becoming inoperable.

(C) It increases fair bargaining.

(D) It leads to better communication.

(82) What are the benefits of downsizing?

(A) Transferring some operations from the company's home country to another, which lowers costs

(B) Lowering operating expenses and making the company easier to maintain

(C) Acquiring more assets for the company

(D) Lower need for data collection and maintenance

(83) An on-the-rise company has decided to increase the work hours from six to nine for all employees, effective immediately.

How should the company handle the grievances caused as a result of this action?

(A) Ask for feedback.

(B) Give the employees a logical reason that the decisions will lead to higher pay.

(C) Properly communicate with employees to work toward a mutual agreement.

(D) Inform the employees about the benefits.

(84) What is not a workplace hazard on a construction site?

(A) Defective or inadequate safety equipment that could lead to physical injuries

(B) Mental stress from having to work for a certain number of hours

(C) Working from heights, if not properly given fall protection

(D) Electrical hazards from live wires and improper equipment

(85) Which of the following are cybersecurity measures?

(A) Installing firewalls and other strong software that can target viruses

(B) Providing employees with training to reduce unsafe acts

(C) Ensuring all employees participate in the safety processes

(D) Making all employees wear PPE to ensure safety

(86) Which of the following is considered illegal per OSHA?

(A) An employee slips and breaks his arm even after being cautioned that the area is unsafe.

(B) An employee accidentally fractures a bone while working and is given money by the employer to not file a complaint.

(C) An employee is given a choice between filing a complaint and resolving it before it's needed.

(D) An employee files a complaint to OSHA about any injury or health hazard issue.

(87) Why do divestitures take longer than acquisitions?

(A) There are more legally complex issues when dealing with divestitures.

(B) They require a greater amount of data.

(C) They need integration.

(D) None of the above.

(88) Which of the following violates union guidelines?

(A) A union provides the employer with written notice of the strike at least ten days in advance, specifying the date and time the strike will begin.

(B) Two parties mutually reach an agreement through good faith that meets the employees' and employer's needs.

(C) The union decides on a mass strike against the company due to a harassment case. This leads to the employees destroying company property.

(D) Two parties decide to bargain and respectfully reach a conclusion that mutually benefits them

(89) What is the role of HR in terms of merging?

(A) Making sure that no benefit is lost for the employer

(B) Aiming for a mutual agreement between the employee and employer

(C) Making sure that employers choose more efficient employees

(D) Ensuring that the talent within the company is retained

(90) After publishing an extraordinary research paper, a student prodigy is offered a job by a multinational company.

What type of visa is the student qualified for?

(A) H visa

(B) O-1 visa

(C) EB employment visa

(D) E non-immigrant visa

Test 1: Answers & Explanations

(1) (B) Hiring, organizing and managing the workforce.

HRM is the process a company undertakes when hiring talent, giving them the necessary training to perform the job and creating a safe workplace that encourages employee engagement and retention.

(2) (A) Talent acquisition, performance management.

Depending on the size and complexity of the business, the structure of the HR department can change. The majority of HR departments deal with talent acquisition and performance management of the workforce.

Talent acquisition deals with attracting and hiring new employees for the company. It may include advertising jobs and sourcing individuals.

(3) (D) Maintaining a positive work environment.

HR departments have the responsibility to make sure there are no disputes between employees and management and that specific rules ensure a positive work environment.

(4) (A) Management style.

Management style is an internal factor that allows firms to manage their style. It refers to the way the top management interacts with employees. Other internal factors could include employee demographics, the structure and the culture of the company.

(5) (A) Kinds of benefits employees may want.

Workers' age, gender, education level and other demographic traits can influence HRM practices since they influence the sorts of perks and programs that employees may desire.

(6) (C) Dividing employees based on criteria like experiences, abilities and skills.

Employee categorization means dividing employees based on criteria like experiences, abilities, skills, etc. It allows companies to pay employees according to the skills and duties they have.

Categorization doesn't work if employees are divided based on the tasks they're assigned (as these can differ from day to day) or on agreements made between employees and managers.

(7) (A) Skilled vs. unskilled.

Several types of employee classification are used in the workplace, such as full time vs. part time, professional vs. entry-level and permanent vs. temporary. All of these are based on specific job aspects, such as hours worked, the length of employment, payment time, etc.

There is no skilled vs. unskilled classification used in the workforce because it would make companies violate laws like ADEA.

(8) (A) It outlines the steps an organization will take to identify, attract and hire new employees.

A recruitment/section plan allows HR to find and attract brand-new employees. It outlines onboarding techniques and strategies that can help the department come into contact and communicate with talent.

(9) (D) Behavioral assessments.

The recruitment/selection plan uses several methods to evaluate talent. It can evaluate candidate reactions to specific workplace simulations and assessments.

Moreover, it uses skills tests, reference checks and behavioral assessments to understand how a candidate behaves in specific situations, such as during emergencies.

(10) (B) Work-life balance.

A retention plan can include information on the steps companies take to ensure their employees stay with them and that they don't leave. Plus, they include information on ways HR can improve work-life balance.

Companies can improve the work-life balance by using flextime, PTO and wellness programs.

(11) (D) All of the above.

Job analysis is gathering and evaluating information about a job's duties, responsibilities, required knowledge, skills and abilities.

(12) (A) Providing training and development.

Job analysis information is often used in recruitment and hiring, training employees to ensure they can do their jobs, designing jobs and restructuring and determining compensation.

(13) (D) All of the above.

Selecting the correct method, finding the purpose of the job analysis and performing data collection are all necessary steps when conducting job analysis. This helps ensure accurate results.

(14) (C) A written document that outlines the requirements of a job within a company.

Job descriptions are detailed descriptions outlining the duties, responsibilities and requirements of specific jobs. They ensure employees know what they're expected to do on a job and that managers know which skills and abilities to look for in job candidates.

(15) (D) All of the above.

Interviews help HR understand if a candidate is a good fit for the job, what a candidate brings to the position and how a candidate works through problems. This information can allow HR to analyze if the candidate can do the job he or she is applying for and whether the individual will be an asset to the company.

(16) (B) Verifying information.

Verifying information can help HR jump-start the onboarding process. It allows them to confirm the information the candidate has provided in the application and ensure the person is a good fit for the role and the company.

(17) (D) Defining the requirements of the job.

HR managers have to define the requirements of the job when preparing for interviews. This helps them make sure they can ask the right questions, develop the right structure and process and create a list of questions that will help them identify a candidate's skill set.

Interviews also help HR managers determine if candidates will be assets to the company.

(18) (B) Increased focus.

When companies want to become the best companies to work for, they need to dedicate time toward achieving their goals and objectives. This means focusing on what works and what doesn't by conducting tests.

It doesn't necessarily mean they should have the most trained employees, the highest success rates in the industry or make continuous product innovations.

(19) (D) Evaluation of performance.

An evaluation of performance helps HR personnel identify what an employee needs to do in a specific job. This evaluation provides insight into a candidate's skill set. It can also help HR understand whether they want to retain the employee and whether investing time and effort into the candidate will yield profits.

(20) (A) Introducing the company to new employees.

The purpose of employee orientation is to introduce the company to new employees. This helps ensure new employees know what they're expected to do and that the company makes sure it's investing in a candidate who will do what he or she was hired for.

(21) (B) Required skills, competencies.

An organizational learning strategy outlines skills and competencies employees should have to help the company achieve its goals. This strategy enables HR to ensure they know what employees need to learn and how they can acquire these skills.

The strategy also helps HR understand how to approach candidates with skill deficiencies without alienating or offending them.

(22) (A) Audience, behavior, condition, degree.

The four components of learning objectives are the audience (who the learning is intended for), behavior (what the learner should be able to do), condition (the context or environment in which the learning will take place) and degree (the level of mastery required).

(23) (D) Functional.

A functional organizational learning strategy promotes specific skills required to expand the company further. It focuses on developing the skills and knowledge necessary to improve a specific area of the business, such as marketing, finance or operations.

(24) (C) Helping employees reach organizational goals.

HR must ensure employees reach organizational goals during training and development if they want to make sure the person can work in the role he or she was hired for.

This can also help HR identify training deficiencies and programs they can create to enable employees to acquire the skills they need to function in their roles.

(25) (A) Make sure the organization functions optimally.

The HR department has to make sure the organization's workforce functions like a well-oiled machine. They can ensure this by keeping an eye on recruitment, hiring, onboarding, employee engagement, training and other employee-specific organizational functions.

(26) (B) Improving the company's overall performance.

An OD program is meant to improve the performance of a company and involves making changes in team leadership, processes and culture. It is a systematic approach to ensure the organization's problems and issues are dealt with.

These programs focus on why issues are happening and create solutions that target the issues instead of working blindly without concrete data.

(27) (C) Versatility.

All OD programs should be versatile so they can meet unexpected challenges like employee resistance and other issues. The best solutions are always versatile because they can respond to challenges before they become problems.

Aside from that, OD programs should focus on the issues they're targeting, even if they're difficult to resolve.

(28) (C) Training the workforce.

The HR department has to train employees to ensure they can perform the job they're hired for. Training helps HR identify deficiencies and areas of improvement in job candidates. It also helps HR understand which candidates are right for the company.

(29) (A) Potential of an applicant.

Candidate assessments help HR understand how well applicants will perform in the job they're applying for. This involves learning the qualifications, skills and experience (specific to the job applied for) of a candidate.

These assessments enable HR to understand whether the candidate is a good fit for the organizational culture and whether the person will be an asset. Candidate assessments may be conducted online and include behavioral, aptitude, personality and skill tests.

(30) (B) Managers for leadership positions.

Managerial on-the-job training and rotation ensure managers are prepared for the positions they're hired for. This training makes sure they are exposed to simulations and real-world examples of scenarios they are expected to make decisions on.

Moreover, managerial training gives managers an opportunity to develop the skills necessary to do their jobs.

(31) (C) Customized training, immediate application.

On-the-job training allows candidates to acquire the skills they need to perform their jobs. For instance, if they need to know specific software like Salesforce, they can get the skills to work with it through on-the-job training.

Similarly, HR can ensure employee engagement, job satisfaction and increase time-to-productivity by providing on-the-job training.

(32) (B) Increments in time.

Since the employer of the multinational company has decided to pay the salary of its employees every month, it has used the increments of time approach.

If the company had used the total rewards approach, it would've paid the employee benefits as well.

(33) (D) All of the above.

Performance pay can encourage employees to perform at their highest level, aid in attracting and retaining top talent and help align employee and organizational objectives. This also incentivizes the employees to maintain an excellent work ethic and give maximum output. Ultimately, this payment method encourages workers to be more productive and give better results.

(34) (D) Bonuses for reaching company-wide targets.

Financial incentives for managers can come in the form of bonuses, stock options and other equity-related rewards, both long term and short term.

These incentives improve the managers' performance, as they will be more determined to push themselves and the workers harder to achieve company goals.

(35) (C) Researching the pay levels of a similar job in the external market.

Salary scales determined by market factors take into account information regarding comparable positions' going rates on the open market. This is beneficial as it maintains a balanced inflow of employees competing for the job. It is illegal for any firm to create a monopoly to compete with its peers.

If the pay is too much compared to the market, it will create discord in the external market as employees will leave other firms for the new well-paid job. This will generate a huge influx of employees whose selection process can be tedious.

(36) (D) Title VII of the Civil Rights Act.

Employment discrimination based on race, color, religion, sex or national origin is illegal per Title VII of the Civil Rights Act of 1964. This act ended racial segregation in workplaces and schools.

(37) (D) Number of employees.

The number of employees shouldn't matter when making a strategic compensation strategy. Its purpose is to set the position of an organization on the job market, the total amount of cash and the rules for setting the base salary.

(38) (C) Promotion of teamwork and cooperation.

Since the major bank has implemented a profit-sharing program for its customer care staff, they'll be able to make sure customer satisfaction ratings are met or exceeded by providing bonuses.

Moreover, they'll be able to promote teamwork and cooperation between their employees because they'll have to achieve their target by collaborating.

(39) (B) Direct compensation.

Direct compensation is when employees get paid money for the time they work or the results they get. This method increases employee morale and satisfaction as the workers know they will be paid for their hard work. So, they will try to put in more work and give extra time to their job.

(40) (B) Employees, a share of the company's profits.

Plans for gain sharing can be made for an individual, a team or an organization. The rewards are based on how much money the company makes, and the employees who helped make money usually get a share.

A pay-for-performance arrangement benefits organizations with multiple teams working on different projects. Any individual or team helping the company achieve its goals faster will get a profit share. This creates healthy competition for workers, giving them optimum performance as a team.

(41) (D) Recognition awards.

Rewards that have no relation to money are considered nonmonetary. Some examples include honors and awards.

Recognition awards are for employees when bonuses or gain/profit sharing is not possible, such as in small businesses with a limited budget. Giving employees recognition for their hard work will help them remain loyal to the firm and work harder in the future.

(42) (A) Money is what motivates people to work.

This is true. Money is the most common way to pay for things and fulfill basic needs and wants. Currency is the backbone of a thriving society as it is used to fulfill basic household needs and in trades and businesses. Providing someone with money is a major factor in their cooperation and loyalty. This increases employee retention and decreases absenteeism.

(43) (C) The equality of rewards within an organization for people in comparable positions.

Internal equity is an approach of paying equally for equal work. Simply put, workers at the same company who perform identical tasks or have similar skill sets receive equivalent pay and benefits.

Any discrimination in pay or benefits due to race, sex or culture is prohibited.

(44) (A) The National Labor Relations Act.

Workers in the private sector have the legal protection to form unions, negotiate contracts collectively and go on strike, according to the NLRA.

Also known as the Wagner Act, this act forbids employers from interfering with employees organizing, forming or assisting a labor organization, or working together to improve the conditions of employment.

(45) (B) Better financial health and happiness at work.

Helping people pay back their loans is easy, productive and profitable. Including a program like this in a benefits package has a high return on investment and requires only a small amount of resources.

Providing benefits like these to employees makes the work appealing. Paying back loans, especially student loans, can be cumbersome, so helping an employee with this will be a mutually beneficial task as this will ensure employee retention.

(46) (A) They are responsible for their work-related taxes.

Income tax and self-employment tax are typically obligatory payments for independent contractors. Taxes are higher for people with a higher annual income. Independent contractors have to pay taxes to the state.

(47) (D) All of the above.

The SWOT analysis is a strategic plan that helps a company identify its strengths and weaknesses. It helps an organization take advantage of beneficial opportunities and avoid possible risks.

A SWOT analysis can help an organization control internal and external factors that affect the future of the company, for example, assets, media coverage, product demand, competitors and more.

(48) (C) Strengths, weaknesses, opportunities and threats.

SWOT stands for strengths, weaknesses, opportunities and threats. These are the controlling factors that help determine the future of a company.

Strengths make the company stand out and include items such as specific products and services, internal resources and tangible assets. On the other hand, weaknesses are the factors that can negatively affect a company, like competitors, substance limitations, unclear propositions, etc.

Opportunities can help a company by increasing demand for products, positive media coverage and lesser competitors. In contrast, threats may cause harm to the company in the future, like changing policies, negative customer reactions/attitudes and negative media coverage.

(49) (B) Assessing the current position.

The SWOT analysis is a strategic plan that helps a company identify its strengths and weaknesses. It helps an organization take upcoming beneficial opportunities and evade upcoming risks.

A SWOT analysis includes the following steps:

- Understanding the vision the company wishes to promote.
- Assessing current position.
- Distributing responsibilities accordingly.
- Evaluating and measuring outcomes and results.

(50) (D) Remaining open to feedback and encouraging team members to participate.

HR takes actions that directly affect the company's future. Organizational communication building is one of the many responsibilities of the members of HR.

Organizational communication can be promoted by various methods that include:

· Promoting a communication-friendly environment.

· Encouraging teams and team members to get involved.

· Being open to feedback and openly giving feedback.

· Promoting face-to-face meetings with different employees.

· Being vigilant to listen for communication's sake, not just solutions.

(51) (A) Weaknesses.

Weaknesses are the factors that can negatively affect a company, like competitors, substance limitations and unclear propositions.

(52) (A) Negative press coverage.

Threats are the factors that may cause harm to the company in the future, like changing policies, negative customer reactions/attitudes and negative media coverage.

(53) (D) All of the above.

Promoting a communication-friendly environment in the company is an important task. This can help strengthen relationships built on trust between the employees and improve employee retention, employee proficiency, etc.

(54) (D) All of the above.

Some types of organizational communication include vertical, horizontal, internal, external, formal and informal.

All of these are the ways the employees interact with each other, with clients/customers and with the company itself.

(55) (B) Informal.

Grapevine communication is a conversation that takes place in a company that does not adhere to a specific format or framework. Because of this, it is known as informal communication.

Normal non-work talk between employees or chats over lunch breaks is known as grapevine communication.

(56) (D) External.

Communication taking place with non-members of the organization, e.g., clients, businesses, suppliers and investors, is known as external communication. A manager talking to clients is external communication.

(57) (A) Matrix.

The matrix structure is based on teams with two reporting managers. One is the functional manager, who directly overlooks and supervises the projects a team is working on.

On the other hand, product managers are responsible for developing, launching and promoting certain products.

(58) (B) Flatarchy.

A flatarchy structure has few or no levels of management. Managers appointed for these companies are the only link between the executives and the employees. It is a hybrid between a hierarchy and a flat-type organization.

(59) (D) Functional structure.

This organization type is comprised of different teams that have specific jobs, e.g., HR is responsible for managing employees and their benefits. Marketing takes care of advertising the company's products. Finance is responsible for managing the budget for products and more.

(60) (C) Divisional structure.

In the divisional structure, multiple teams are working toward one specific goal. Each team will have its own managers and finances, forming semi-autonomous working units. An example of this type of structure includes chain food restaurants that create divisions and branches based on location.

(61) (B) Flatarchy.

In a flatarchy, employees are free to pitch new ideas for the company and its products. A flatarchy structure has few or no levels of management.

(62) (D) All of the above.

HRIS is the software responsible for maintaining the HR functions of an organization. Some of its functions include the following:

· Data management.

· Recruitment and hiring.

· Performance management.

· Learning management.

· Compensation and benefits.

· Time and attendance.

(63) (D) Employee retention.

Employee retention is not the responsibility of HRIS. HRIS is responsible for data management, recruitment and lean management.

(64) (C) That support tactical goals.

The operational goals include time-bound, day-to-day objectives that need to be performed accordingly. These goals are usually department, finance or product specifications and support the tactical objectives of an organization.

(65) (D) Both (A) and (B).

HR operations and goals include day-to-day tasks that support the overall HR functions. These include short-term and long-term plans for the company.

(66) (A) Guidelines for managing employees and internal issues.

HR policies are the guidelines provided to HR members to manage employees and to manage other internal issues of the company.

(67) (B) Steps HR must follow to manage employee relations and administration.

HR procedures are the outlines provided to HR to manage employees and administer their relations. HR policies are also provided within these procedures.

(68) (D) All of the above.

The HR policies, procedures and operations provide guidelines on the treatment of employees and other HR functions, such as employee management, training and more.

(69) (C) Give recognition to employees who work harder.

The organization can reward any individual who stands out in the company. This will motivate the employees to work harder for the recognition of the company and their superiors.

(70) (B) The Davis-Bacon Act.

The Davis-Bacon Act is intended to prevent contractors from driving down wages in a particular area by paying workers less than the prevailing wage.

It also ensures that the federal government, as a major construction contractor, is not contributing to the suppression of wages in a particular region.

(71) (B) The Taft-Hartley Act.

The Taft-Hartley Act balances the interests of employers and employees by implementing restrictions on labor unions, like prohibitions on secondary boycotts, sympathy strikes and union contributions to political campaigns.

The act also gives employers more rights to free speech during labor disputes and allows states to create right-to-work laws that prohibit mandatory union membership as a condition of employment.

(72) (A) According to OSHA, the company's decision could end up causing issues due to defective equipment.

The decision is incorrect. Defective equipment can pose safety hazards to the user or those in the vicinity. For example, a defective electrical appliance could cause electrocution, or a faulty gas appliance could cause a gas leak and subsequent explosion.

(73) (B) FACT is an amendment to improve accuracy, whereas FRCA is a federal law regulating credit information.

The Fair and Accurate Credit Transactions Act, also known as FACT, is an amendment that was passed to increase the accuracy of a consumer's credit record and details related to the credit card. It allows consumers to obtain a copy of their files from the agency once a year.

The Fair Reporting Credit Act, also known as FRCA, is a federal law passed to regulate consumers' credit information and other related reports. This act was proposed to assure consumers that their privacy was maintained.

(74) (B) Writing a review on the potential dangers of taking the medicine.

This is a safety measure for the product, but not the workplace environment. Writing such a review will not prevent any dangers within the workplace.

(75) (D) Discuss and create an effective business continuity plan in case of an emergency.

The business continuity plan discusses countermeasures for emergency events, such as the national crisis over the pandemic.

(76) (A) When a female employee's pay is deducted despite her taking a paid leave due to being pregnant.

The Equal Pay Act of 1963 ensures that all employees are treated the same based on their work efficiency. This allows women to be treated equally to their male colleagues in the working environment.

(77) (A) The Rehabilitation Act of 1973.

The Rehabilitation Act of 1973 was passed to provide accessibility to a company for disabled people.

(78) (C) Aggressive tactical bargaining.

When an employer threatens retaliation if a union doesn't accept their proposal, they conduct aggressive tactical bargaining, which is when one party uses strong-arm tactics to gain leverage over the other party.

(79) (A) They provide a workforce analysis of the organization.

HR is responsible for analyzing the workforce within the organization and providing this information to sustain the company.

(80) (B) The employee is likely to have repetitive motion disorder.

If the employee is working ten hours every day, he or she might end up with muscle, tendon and nerve injuries, which are associated with repetitive motions like typing and using a mouse.

(81) (D) It leads to better communication.

Business integration can lead to better communication between teams and employees. It doesn't prevent companies from becoming inoperable or increase fair bargaining capacity.

(82) (B) Lowering operating expenses and making the company easier to maintain.

Downsizing allows HR to lower business operation expenses and make the company easier to manage. It also increases return on investment and time-to-productivity.

(83) (C) Properly communicate with employees to work toward a mutual agreement.

If the start-up has decided to initiate a nine-hour workweek, it can handle resulting grievances by properly communicating with employees and ensuring they know why they have to work for so long.

After that, it should keep employees informed about the status of the investigation and any decisions or actions taken in response to the grievance. This can help build trust and reduce frustration.

(84) (B) Mental stress from having to work for a certain number of hours.

Although mental stress is a workplace health hazard, this is linked to a construction site specifically and could be applicable in any workplace.

(85) (A) Installing firewalls and other strong software that can target viruses.

A firewall protects devices and prevents third-party viruses from attacking and harming computers.

(86) (B) An employee accidentally fractures a bone while working and is given money by the employer to not file a complaint.

OSHA requires that any work-related injury must be reported and recorded. Not recording a work-related injury is illegal.

(87) (B) They require a greater amount of data.

Divestiture is more complex because businesses have to deal with reassigning the employees who work for them.

(88) (C) The union decides on a mass strike against the company due to a harassment case. This leads to the employees destroying company property.

Before a strike can occur, all legal requirements, such as obtaining authorization from the union or complying with notice and cooling-off period requirements, must be met. Not only that, but the strike cannot damage property.

(89) (D) Ensuring that the talent within the company is retained.

HR ensures that the company still has talented employees. This will improve efficiency and make the merger much more successful.

(90) (B) O-1 visa.

The O-1 visa is appropriate for a student with extraordinary talents who has become internationally recognized in art, science, education, business or athletics.

Test 2: Questions

(1) How is personnel management different from HRM?

(A) HRM uses a strategic approach, and PM takes an administrative one.

(B) PM treats workers as an essential company asset; HRM treats them as machines.

(C) PM focuses on employee relations, whereas HRM focuses on employee training.

(D) None of the above.

(2) HR guides an organization's ____________, ____________ and __________.

(A) Management, regulation, systems

(B) Mission statement, goals, planning

(C) Budget, employee requirements, mission

(D) Vision, mission, values

(3) The values of an organization define/ensure a company's ____________.

(A) Future state

(B) Processes align with its goals

(C) Culture and shape its behavior

(D) None of the above

(4) HR can help develop company vision by ________.

(A) Introducing training programs

(B) Developing policies that always reflect their parent company's goals

(C) Promoting a positive and ethical workplace

(D) None of the above

(5) Sourcing internal talent refers to ________.

(A) Attracting employees with the skills to fill newly created roles within a company

(B) Utilizing skill assessments to determine job applicants' or current employees' skills

(C) Outlining the responsibilities of a specific job within a company

(D) All of the above

(6) Sourcing external talent refers to _________.

(A) Identifying and attracting workers outside a company

(B) Identifying and attracting workers from inside a company

(C) Using job analysis to find workers

(D) None of the above

(7) A transfer happens when employees __________.

(A) Come back to work for a company

(B) Move from one role or department within a company

(C) Both (A) and (B)

(D) None of the above

(8) MSP is an acronym for __________.

(A) Managed Service Products

(B) Methods of Service Providers

(C) Managed Service Providers

(D) None of the above

(9) Contractor payrolling is also known as a/an:

(A) Employer of record

(B) Temporary-to-permanent program

(C) Payrolling service

(D) Both (A) and (C)

(10) What is a cognitive ability test?

(A) This type of test targets manual labor required for the job.

(B) This type of test measures an individual's characteristics and tendencies

(C) This type of test assesses a candidate's mental abilities.

(D) All of the above

(11) What are the benefits of using work samples and simulations?

(A) Improved accuracy

(B) Objective evaluation

(C) Increased candidate engagement

(D) All of the above

(12) What is the purpose of management assessment centers?

(A) To give promotions to staff who work the longest hours

(B) To determine a candidate's suitability for a management role and to identify the person's strengths and areas for development

(C) To determine a candidate's mental condition

(D) None of the above

(13) Key considerations while preparing for an interview include _______.

(A) Data collection

(B) Verifying information

(C) Providing company knowledge

(D) Defining the job requirements

(14) HR professionals can reduce the risk of turnover by _______.

(A) Ensuring they select the best candidate

(B) Improving the organization's overall success

(C) Hiring more workers

(D) Offering higher wages

(15) A/An _______ is used in the high-volume recruitment process.

(A) Unstructured interview

(B) Structured interview

(C) Semi-structured interview

(D) Mock interview

(16) In a/an __________, the interviewer does not follow predetermined questions.

(A) Mock interview

(B) Structured interview

(C) Unstructured interview

(D) Behavioral interview

(17) Which statement is false about unstructured interviews?

(A) It involves open-ended questions.

(B) It comes after the predetermined set of questions.

(C) It usually has a more relaxed setting.

(D) It holds a better flow of conversation.

(18) What is the ADDIE model?

(A) A methodology for developing training

(B) A type of on-the-job training

(C) A technique for breaking down complex information

(D) A system for online learning

(19) Which step of the ADDIE model involves generating learning resources with media support?

(A) Analysis

(B) Design

(C) Development

(D) Evaluation

(20) What is the primary advantage of programmed learning?

(A) It reduces the cost of training.

(B) It allows employees to learn anytime, anywhere.

(C) It provides in-time training with operational experience.

(D) It allows learners to comfortably learn at their own pace.

(21) What is the purpose of chunking?

(A) To make learning and retaining information easier

(B) To provide in-time training

(C) To increase individual knowledge and proficiency

(D) To simulate a real working environment

(22) Vestibule training focuses on ________ training.

(A) Employee job education

(B) Simulated cockpit

(C) Zoom meeting

(D) Skilled

(23) _____________ training involves HR working to improve work motivation, employee confidence and productivity.

(A) On-the-job

(B) Apprenticeship

(C) Informal

(D) Job instruction

(24) The purpose of team training is to ___________.

(A) Reduce the cost of training

(B) Make time management easier

(C) Increase employee knowledge

(D) Increase overall performance

(25) Job rotation is a method that involves ___________.

(A) Off-the-job training

(B) One-on-one development

(C) Employees moving from one job to another within the organization

(D) Employees being paired with a more experienced colleague to learn the skills and responsibilities required for a specific role

(26) The goal of job rotation is to provide employees with ___________.

(A) Broad-based experience and exposure to different areas of the organization

(B) A safe and supportive environment to explore new ideas

(C) Ways to solve real-world problems through a collaborative process

(D) Work tasks or projects outside their typical job responsibilities

(27) Coaching is a strategy where employees _________.

(A) Are moved from one job to another within the organization for a specified period of time

(B) Are paired with a more experienced colleague to learn the skills and responsibilities required for a specific role

(C) Have a coach who teaches them the ropes

(D) Solve real-world problems through a collaborative process

(28) The understudy approach is a type of off-the-job training method where an employee is __________.

(A) Paired with a more experienced colleague to learn the skills and responsibilities required for a specific role

(B) Given a task that is outside the person's typical job responsibilities

(C) Provided a coach

(D) None of the above

(29) Action learning happens when an employee ____________.

(A) Solves real-world problems through a simulation

(B) Works with a coach to improve their skill set

(C) Is moved from one job to another within the organization

(D) Is paired with a more experienced colleague

(30) A stretch assignment is a type of training method that allows employees to learn _______.

(A) Job skills from team leaders

(B) How to work with supervisors

(C) How to work on complex tasks

(D) How to solve real-world problems through simulations

(31) Outside seminars are a type of training method that involves _______.

(A) A one-on-one relationship between a coach and a trainee

(B) Employees solving real-world problems within a team

(C) Employees learning how to do their jobs in training sessions that take place outside an organization

(D) None of the above

(32) A _______________ is a type of incentive pay program linked to a company's strategic goals.

(A) Pay system

(B) Profit-sharing program

(C) Fixed salary payment system

(D) Time-based compensation system

(33) The point method involves _______.

(A) Grades based on how challenging a task is, how much responsibility it requires and what skills it needs

(B) Points based on responsibility, skills, effort and working conditions

(C) Software systems that analyze the duties, responsibilities and requirements of different organizational positions

(D) None of the above

(34) Employees are compensated through ___________ and ___________.

(A) Base salary, wages

(B) Direct, indirect compensation

(C) Primary, secondary compensation

(D) Bonuses, commissions

(35) Incentive pay rewards employees ___________.

(A) With a fixed salary depending on their job title and responsibilities

(B) Depending on their organizational ranking

(C) For reaching certain objectives or goals

(D) According to the number of hours worked

(36) The localization approach to compensation sets pay levels based on _________.

(A) A one-size-fits-all method

(B) How much it costs to live and how the market performs in each location

(C) Rewards and benefits that don't involve money

(D) How long employees have worked for a company

(37) A law firm won a big celebrity case and decided to give employees a huge raise and a couple of benefits like exclusive gym membership and an executive retreat.

Which HR approach did the law firm use?

(A) Comparable worth

(B) Broadbanding

(C) Broad oversight of executive pay

(D) Total rewards program

(38) Why do employers need to assign a new pay scale?

(A) Because the employees made good sales

(B) To ensure employees are paid fairly for their job duties and responsibilities

(C) Because the results of a salary survey of people working a similar job show that the pay rate of that particular job is higher

(D) Both (B) and (C)

(39) Merit pay is a system that rewards employees _________.

(A) Depending on the number of products they create or the number of jobs they complete

(B) Depending on their performance or achievements

(C) For achieving specific goals or outcomes

(D) Depending on their organizational seniority

(40) Inequity in team recognition programs can be caused by __________.

(A) Regularly recognizing employees who go above and beyond their job responsibilities

(B) Recognizing employees who reach or surpass organizational goals, regardless of their team contributions

(C) Giving employees equal opportunities to comment on their peers' performance

(D) Recognizing employees who take time off frequently for self-care and mental health

(41) Sarah got injured at work and needs to see a doctor. Her employer pays for her medical bills through worker's compensation insurance.

Will Sarah have to pay out of pocket for her health care?

(A) Yes, she will have to pay out of pocket for her health care.

(B) No, her medical bills will be paid for by her worker's compensation insurance.

(C) Her employer will pay for some of her health care costs but not all of them

(D) None of the above

(42) Which of the following is not a purpose of severance pay?

(A) To financially help workers who are losing their jobs

(B) To give employees a reason to leave the company on their own

(C) To stop terminated employees from going to court

(D) To show appreciation to long-term employees

(43) Which of the following represents a part of a total rewards approach to pay?

(A) It focuses mostly on salary and bonuses as the main forms of payment.

(B) It includes financial and non-financial rewards, like recognition programs and flexible work hours.

(C) It pays people based on the jobs they do.

(D) It gives employees perks based on how long they've worked for the company.

(44) What is an example of a defined contribution retirement plan?

(A) 401(k) plan

(B) Pension plan

(C) Social Security

(D) None of the above

(45) Which of the following is usually deducted from an employee's gross pay?

(A) Bonus

(B) Pay for performance

(C) Tax

(D) Overtime pay

(46) A broadband pay structure may _________.

(A) Be too hard to manage and explain to employees

(B) Be too inflexible to adapt to the job market or business environment changes

(C) Be too competitive to attract top talent

(D) Squeeze salaries into the same general range

(47) Effective strategic planning for employee engagement can help boost ____________.

(A) Employee retention

(B) Employee proficiency

(C) Employee satisfaction

(D) All of the above

(48) What is the primary cause of a lack of employee engagement?

(A) Conducting year-round surveys in the company

(B) Keeping track of employee engagement

(C) Providing the employees with proper resources

(D) Not helping employees with difficult tasks

(49) What is the best way to increase employee engagement?

(A) Promote communication and encourage employees to give feedback

(B) Establish strict rules that no employee can take charge autonomously

(C) Maintain silence in the office building

(D) Give feedback to the employees but don't follow their suggestions

(50) Employee engagement is the connection employees _________.

(A) Feel with their employers

(B) Have with their work and the tasks they perform

(C) Have to the organization they work in

(D) All of the above

(51) Sienna's team is falling behind other teams in the department. Seeing her team struggle, she decides to conduct a survey to understand why people in her team are struggling with their responsibilities.

Sienna has made use of ____________ skills.

(A) Employee retention

(B) Employee engagement

(C) Problem-solving

(D) None of the above

(52) HR can improve employee retention by ____________.

(A) Allowing employees to do as they want

(B) Making employees feel valued

(C) Allowing employees to figure out problems by themselves

(D) All of the above

(53) The ____________ department is responsible for increasing employee engagement.

(A) HR

(B) Finance

(C) Marketing

(D) R&D

(54) HR can measure employee engagement by ______.

(A) Asking employees how they feel

(B) Asking managers what they feel about their employees

(C) Conducting surveys and interviews

(D) None of the above

(55) ___________ interviews involve managers asking employees about their previous work experience.

(A) Coding

(B) Panel

(C) Unstructured

(D) Off-site

(56) A/an ________ interview involves an employer questioning an employee about his or her work by using predefined questions.

(A) Unstructured

(B) Stressful

(C) Structured

(D) Improvised

(57) Jack has a successful career and a healthy family life. Which of the following best describes his situation?

(A) Work/family balance

(B) Work/life balance

(C) Work/home balance

(D) Work/spouse balance

(58) Sarah works a remote job at a company. She failed to submit her upcoming project on time during her regular work hours and didn't pick up her phone when called.

Which of the following is Sarah practicing?

(A) Work/life balance

(B) Setting boundaries

(C) Negligence and noncompliance

(D) None of the above

(59) Job sharing, remote working and telecommuting are all examples of __________.

(A) Alternative work arrangements

(B) Setting boundaries

(C) Work-from-home schemes

(D) Flexible working

(60) Working for more hours in a day but fewer days a week is known as ________.

(A) Condensed work

(B) Flextime

(C) Hybrid work

(D) Shift work

(61) ___________ work refers to working specific hours in a day.

(A) Condensed

(B) Flextime

(C) Hybrid

(D) Shift

(62) In Alanna's firm, employees are free to work anytime they want, provided they do their work on time.

Which of the following types of work does Alanna's company use?

(A) Condensed work

(B) Flextime

(C) Hybrid work

(D) Shift work

(63) A recent data report showed that a company had 50 on-site working employees and 25 who worked off-site/remotely.

The company has which of the following work arrangements?

(A) Condensed

(B) Flextime

(C) Hybrid

(D) Shift

(64) Jack went on vacation on December 20 after working for two consecutive years without PTO. However, his company had an emergency on December 22 and called him to ask for assistance.

Jack didn't respond when called.

Which of the following best describes Jack's behavior?

(A) He is ensuring that he has an adequate work/life balance.

(B) He is setting boundaries.

(C) He is showing negligence and noncompliance.

(D) All of the above.

(65) ________________ and ______________ aren't steps in implementing an employee engagement plan.

(A) Allocating budget, finances

(B) Selecting a leadership team, ensuring they can do their job

(C) Making sure the employee engagement plan follows the organization's rules, vision

(D) Allotting all employees free time every second week, ensuring they adhere to it

(66) Kieran works at a corporation that provides consulting services. His company decides to increase employee engagement through a bring-your-child-to-work day.

Kieran's company has used which of the following strategies?

(A) Family-friendly policies

(B) Work-from-home schemes

(C) Alternative working arrangement

(D) Flexible working

(67) Organizational success depends on ____________________.

(A) Increasing employee engagement

(B) Ensuring customer satisfaction

(C) Creating effective financial plans

(D) All of the above

(68) Employee engagement can decrease if companies ________.

(A) Empower employees

(B) Increase team communication

(C) Disrespect employees and their boundaries

(D) Give feedback

(69) Which act prohibits most private employers from using lie detector tests for pre-employment screening or during employment?

(A) The Dodd-Frank Wall Street Reform and Consumer Protection Act

(B) The Employee Polygraph Protection Act

(C) The Davis-Bacon Act

(D) The Electronic Communications Privacy Act

(70) What does the Equal Pay Act protect against?

(A) Wage disparity based on gender

(B) Discrimination against individuals with disabilities

(C) Workplace harassment

(D) Discrimination based on race

(71) Which of the following acts regulate the collection of consumers' credit information and credit reports?

(A) The Copeland "Anti-kickback" Act

(B) The Fair and Accurate Credit Transactions Act

(C) The Equal Credit Opportunity Act

(D) The Consumer Credit Protection Act

(72) Under which law can the IRS impose penalties on an individual involved in an excessively beneficial transaction?

(A) The Immigration and Nationality Act of 1952

(B) The Immigration Reform and Control Act of 1986

(C) The IRS Intermediate Sanctions of 2002

(D) The Labor Management Relations Act of 1947

(73) What is the primary purpose of the National Labor Relations Act of 1935?

(A) To prohibit employers from interfering with employees' rights to organize into trade unions and engage in bargaining and strikes

(B) To establish national standards to protect sensitive health information from being disclosed without the knowledge or consent of the patient

(C) To prohibit any payout to foreign officials

(D) To impose penalties on an individual involved in an excessively beneficial transaction

(74) Which of the following employment losses are covered by the Worker Adjustment and Retraining Notification Act (1988)?

(A) Layoffs exceeding three months

(B) Terminations due to poor performance

(C) Layoffs exceeding six months

(D) Reductions in employees' work hours of less than 50% during any six months

(75) The purpose of the Civil Service Reform Act (1978) is to allow ________.

(A) Federal employees to organize, bargain collectively and participate in labor organizations

(B) The regulation of the flow of people and products into and out of the country

(C) The development of employment laws

(D) The governance of the collection, maintenance, use and dissemination of personal information maintained in the records of federal agencies

(76) The difference between a closed shop arrangement and an agency shop arrangement is that only __________.

(A) Union members can be employed in a closed shop, while non-union members must pay union dues in an agency shop

(B) Non-union members must pay union dues in a closed shop, while union members can be employed in an agency shop

(C) Non-union members are not required to join the union in a closed shop, while they are required to join the union in an agency shop

(D) Union members are given hiring preference in a closed shop, while non-union members are given hiring preference in an agency shop

(77) Employee engagement ________ the likelihood of unionization, while unionization _________ employee engagement.

(A) Reduces, increases

(B) Increases, decreases

(C) Balances, balances

(D) Decreases, decreases

(78) _____________ is the first step in the union drive and election process.

(A) Holding a hearing

(B) Obtaining authorization cards

(C) Engaging in the campaign

(D) Making initial contact

(79) Which of the following is a key strike guideline?

(A) Being respectful and professional

(B) Peacefully protesting

(C) Prioritizing mutual interests

(D) Holding a hearing

(80) What is the first step to handling a grievance situation?

(A) Investigating the situation

(B) Following the grievance procedure

(C) Remaining impartial

(D) Listening to the employee

(81) You should ________________ the situation if the grievance involves an alleged violation of the contract or company policies.

(A) Ignore

(B) Investigate

(C) Make assumptions about

(D) Take sides in

(82) Creating a safe workplace can reduce employee ________.

(A) Productivity

(B) Accidents and injuries

(C) Morale and productivity

(D) Loyalty and turnover rates

(83) The top management ensures that employees are __________.

(A) Resistant to following safety protocols

(B) Working in and implementing a safety culture within the organization

(C) Not trained to recognize and respond to potential hazards

(D) Regularly overlooking and ignoring workplace hazards

(84) Supervisors must ensure that employees ________.

(A) Work in unsafe conditions

(B) Report all accidents and near-miss incidents

(C) Report any safety concerns or hazards they encounter

(D) None of the above

(85) The first step in securing a workplace is ___________.

(A) Installing mechanical, natural and organizational security systems

(B) Reviewing potential threats

(C) Performing a risk assessment

(D) Giving training to employees

(86) Employers can prevent workplace exposure to infectious diseases by __________.

(A) Developing employee assistance programs

(B) Providing ergonomic workstations

(C) Promoting good hygiene

(D) Limiting the time employees spend performing repetitive tasks

(87) Organizational change is a company's plan to ________.

(A) Alter its fundamental elements, including its practices, culture, workforce, offerings, infrastructure and technological advancements

(B) Increase revenue without altering its fundamental elements

(C) Decrease expenses without altering its fundamental elements

(D) Hire brand-new employees without altering its fundamental elements

(88) Business continuity management is the ________________ and preparation done to guarantee that an organization can carry out its essential business tasks in an emergency.

(A) Reactive planning

(B) Proactive planning

(C) Instructive planning

(D) Rushed planning

(89) Business integration is when a corporation ________.

(A) Unifies its various technical models to ensure they align and sync with the corporate culture

(B) Sells off a sizable portion of its assets

(C) Dissolves a sizable portion of its assets

(D) Hires new employees

(90) Who can receive a dependent E visa?

(A) The spouses and children (under 21) of treaty traders, treaty investors or employees of enterprises

(B) Individuals with extraordinary abilities in science or arts

(C) Athletes and their coaches or support staff

(D) Aliens with outstanding professors and researchers

Test 2: Answers & Explanations

(1) (A) HRM uses a strategic approach, and PM takes an administrative one.

Personnel management is a branch of management that deals with hiring, staffing, training, compensating and developing the workforce to accomplish organizational goals.

On the other hand, HR management deals with searching for, retaining, developing and coordinating people at work in a way that will get the most out of them.

(2) (D) Vision, mission, values.

HR helps ensure a company can achieve its mission, goals and vision while adhering to its values.

(3) (C) Culture and shape its behavior.

Company values are what your company believes in. They help make sure a company keeps to specific principles that form the foundation of the company culture.

(4) (B) Developing policies that always reflect their parent company's goals.

HR can encourage the development of the vision of an organization by developing policies that always reflect the parent company's goals. This vision will help everybody in the company work toward a single goal, ensuring success and business growth.

(5) (A) Attracting employees with the skills to fill newly created roles within a company.

Finding and attracting personnel with the ability to fill a vacant position is known as sourcing internal talent. It is a useful tactic for businesses to create a solid and competent team.

(6) (A) Identifying and attracting workers outside a company.

Finding and luring job prospects from outside a business to fill open positions is known as sourcing external talent.

(7) (B) Move from one role or department within a company.

Employees that move to another department or job inside an organization undergo a transfer. Relocating staff members may bring a plethora of expertise to the new position, easing the transition for both the person and the company.

(8) (C) Managed Service Providers.

MSP stands for Managed Service Providers. MSPs are third-party companies that businesses use to hire candidates. Small businesses and nonprofit or government organizations like employment agencies use MSPs.

(9) (D) Both (A) and (C).

Employing independent contractors or freelancers through contractor payrolling, often known as "employer of record" or "payrolling services," is a common practice.

(10) (C) This type of test assesses a candidate's mental abilities.

Cognitive exams are used to evaluate an applicant's mental faculties, including memory and problem-solving skills. They are employed in technical fields.

(11) (D) All of the above.

The use of simulations and work samples leads to enhanced candidate involvement, objective evaluation and improved accuracy.

(12) (B) To determine a candidate's suitability for a management role and to identify the person's strengths and areas for development.

Job candidates' skills and talents are assessed using work samples and simulations in either a real-world or simulated setting. They frequently serve as a supplement to established techniques like interviews and résumé reviews during the hiring process.

(13) (D) Defining the job requirements.

While getting ready for interviews, key preparations include defining the job requirements. Assessing candidates' abilities, capacities and social fit with the association is also fundamental.

(14) (A) Ensuring they select the best candidate.

HR professionals can ensure that they select the best candidate for the position by following a structured interview procedure, lowering the likelihood of employee turnover and enhancing the organization's overall success.

(15) (B) Structured interview.

In a structured interview, each candidate is consistently assessed by the interviewer as they follow a predetermined set of questions. When several candidates are being interviewed for a single post during high-volume recruiting procedures, this style of interview is frequently employed.

Structured interviews can aid in removing subjectivity and biases from the interviewing process.

(16) (C) Unstructured interview.

An unstructured interview allows the conversation to flow more naturally since the interviewer does not stick to a set of predetermined questions. This allows the interviewer to learn more about a candidate's motivation, personality and communication abilities.

Open-ended questions may be used in an informal interview to give applicants a chance to speak freely and naturally about their qualifications.

(17) (B) It comes after the predetermined set of questions.

This is false. In an unstructured meeting, the questioner doesn't follow predetermined questions.

(18) (A) A methodology for developing training.

ADDIE is a method for systematically developing training. The model's five phases are denoted by the acronym ADDIE, which stands for analysis, design, development, implementation and evaluation.

(19) (C) Development.

The development phase is part of the ADDIE model that involves making learning resources with media support. Based on the specifications from the design phase, training materials are created in this phase.

The creation of learning objectives, the selection of appropriate media and technologies, and the design and production of training materials are all part of the development phase.

(20) (D) It allows learners to comfortably learn at their own pace.

Programmed learning is an independent, individualized way for students to progress through the material at their own speed.

(21) (A) To make learning and retaining information easier.

The reason for chunking is to make learning and retaining data simpler. Chunking includes separating complex data into smaller pieces, or "chunks." This diminishes the mental burden and upgrades working memory, which is helpful to students.

(22) (A) Employee job education.

Vestibule training focuses on employee job education. It utilizes materials that are indistinguishable from those utilized in the real workplace. It is intended to give people active experience and practice in a controlled setting before they enter the workforce.

(23) (A) On-the-job.

On-the-job training involves HR working to improve work motivation, employee confidence and productivity. It is a type of training that takes place while employees are performing their regular job duties.

(24) (D) Increase overall performance.

Team training can increase overall business performance, allowing managers to meet goals faster and improve time-to-productivity. It does this by ensuring adequate communication, collaboration and coordination between employees.

Team training can also improve team effectiveness and allow for better business outcomes, such as higher ROI, improved employee engagement and increased company loyalty.

(25) (C) Employees moving from one job to another within the organization.

Job rotation is a method in which HR moves employees from one department or another because they can better fill that spot. Job rotation can help employees learn new skills that can enable upward mobility in the organization. So, job rotation is also a strategy for innovation in the company.

(26) (A) Broad-based experience and exposure to different areas of the organization.

Job rotation happens when HR shifts employees to another department so that they can acquire new skills and help struggling departments reach targets. It helps employees experience working with other teams and provides them with exposure to other departments of the organization.

For instance, if a supply chain manager is moved into marketing, the employee can learn how to create marketing campaigns and reach new audiences.

(27) (C) Have a coach who teaches them the ropes.

Coaching is a strategy where employees are mentored by another employee with more experience in whatever job they've signed up for. For example, an HR executive will be mentored by an HR manager, while a sales associate will be coached by their supervisor.

This strategy encourages collaboration between team members and enables the upward flow of information as well as encourages information retention.

(28) (A) Paired with a more experienced colleague to learn the skills and responsibilities required for a specific role.

The understudy approach takes place when an employee studies under a more experienced employee, such as a manager, supervisor or team leader. The experienced employee helps the new candidate learn the ropes of the job, e.g., understanding what's expected and learning the necessary skills and responsibilities.

(29) (A) Solves real-world problems through a simulation.

Action learning happens when employees work through a real-world problem either on the job or through simulations. For instance, an HR executive can learn how to work with agitated employees through a real-world simulation based on a real example.

Similarly, a sales executive might learn how to cold call by shadowing a more experienced employee in a real-world customer-to-business (C2B) or business-to-business (B2B) interaction.

(30) (C) How to work on complex tasks.

Stretch assignments challenge employees by giving them complex tasks that are above their current level. They allow employees to upskill and learn ways to perform tasks they haven't done before, such as learning a specific software. These assignments can help employees move to other departments as well.

(31) (C) Employees learning how to do their jobs in training sessions that take place outside an organization.

An outside seminar is a training method that helps employees learn about current industry trends and best practices. They are led by industry experts and encourage upskilling.

(32) (B) Profit-sharing program.

Profit-sharing programs are incentive programs linked to a company's strategic goals. They give employees a share in a company's profits. They're deferred plans, which means they reward employees at retirement. That means they require employees to work with companies for life.

Some companies also share profits with employees whenever they leave, but they have terms for accessing these schemes.

(33) (B) Points based on responsibility, skills, effort and working conditions.

The point method gives points to jobs based on factors like effort, skill and responsibility. These factors are specific to each company, depending on industry relevance. This method helps HR understand responsibilities common to jobs being evaluated, allowing them to create job descriptions.

For instance, a managerial position might be given a 4 out of 5 because it requires more time and skills to perform. However, an intern position might be given 1 point because it doesn't take much skill or time to perform.

A point-based job evaluation helps HR understand which jobs require more compensation and training. It also enables the department to make sure they have the necessary resources to provide assistance to struggling employees at every level.

(34) (B) Direct, indirect compensation.

Companies typically compensate employees through direct and indirect compensation. The former rewards employees through financial means, such as salary, commissions and bonuses, and the latter ensures compensation through non-financial means like awards, PTO, etc.

Direct reward systems encourage employees to work harder because they know they'll be compensated more for what they're doing. Non-financial reward systems have a similar effect by ensuring employees are recognized for their efforts at work.

So, both these reward systems increase engagement and job satisfaction, allowing organizations to meet goals and targets beforehand.

(35) (C) For reaching certain objectives or goals.

Incentive pay includes both direct and indirect compensation, such as gross salary, benefits, bonuses, commissions, etc. This compensation type urges employees to meet targets faster, increasing time-to-completion and time-to-productivity. It also increases employee engagement, which is the hallmark of business success.

(36) (B) How much it costs to live and how the market performs in each location.

The localization approach to compensation allows HR to understand how much a certain market pays for a specific skill. For instance, if a corporation is migrating its operations to Asia, it will have to understand how much each employee is paid in that region of the world.

If the company doesn't do this, it might spend more than it gets back, which will be bad for business. In these situations, HR can use the localization approach to ensure they pay slightly higher salaries to ensure employees gravitate to their company.

(37) (D) Total rewards program.

When the law firm decided to give its employees a raise and benefits, it used the total rewards approach, which is when employees meet or exceed company targets and are rewarded for their work.

The total rewards program also encourages employee engagement and higher job satisfaction, which translates to increased employee loyalty and higher ROI for the business.

(38) (D) Both (B) and (C).

Employers need to assign a new pay scale when they find that the market is paying more for similar jobs.

For instance, if an employer is paying $90,000 per year to a project manager and they conduct their annual pay scale survey and find out that the pay in the market has increased due to inflation, they may increase the pay of their employees to ensure they don't leave.

(39) (C) For achieving specific goals or outcomes.

Merit pay is a system that pays employees based on achieved business goals and targets. For instance, a salesperson will be paid a commission or bonus for meeting or exceeding monthly targets.

This encourages employees to work harder to achieve their goals, increases loyalty and improves customer satisfaction, leading to business growth.

(40) (B) Recognizing employees who reach or surpass organizational goals, regardless of their team contributions.

Acknowledgment for an individual's accomplishment and not the other team members who may have helped that person succeed can lead to sentiments of anger, jealousy and low morale.

No company can succeed without teamwork, and the building block of teamwork is trust and equity, where all team members are appreciated.

(41) (B) No, her medical bills will be paid for by her worker's compensation insurance.

Because Sarah's medical insurance bills are covered by her employer, her bills will be paid by her insurance.

Some companies provide worker's compensation insurance as a benefit for their employees in case of any injury or loss. The money is either drawn from the company's collective fund or directly from a separate fund especially kept for insurance purposes.

(42) (D) To show appreciation to long-term employees.

This is not a purpose of severance pay. Severance pay is usually given to employees in case of job termination or forced resignation. This fund is to help employees who are losing their jobs.

(43) (B) It includes financial and non-financial rewards, like recognition programs and flexible work hours.

Total rewards programs are programs where incentives are either monetary or nonmonetary or, in some cases, both, and are given to employees based on their achievements.

The total rewards approach is a massive driving factor for employees as they can get monetary benefits such as financial rewards and insurance and nonmonetary benefits such as recognition and a flexible work schedule with paid leave.

This leads to employee retention, high morale, motivation to reach the company's targets, low absenteeism, higher productivity and much more.

(44) (A) 401(k) plan.

A 401(k) is a type of defined contribution retirement plan in which employees can choose to put aside a certain amount of their salary each month as a part of their retirement plan.

(45) (C) Tax.

Taxes are usually deducted from an employee's salary to pay for government programs and services like education, health care, infrastructure, social security and defense.

Most of the time, these taxes go to the federal, state and local governments. They are used to pay for public goods and services that help the whole community.

(46) (D) Squeeze salaries into the same general range.

Broadband pay structures tend to have fewer pay grades and salary ranges than traditional ones, making it harder for some employees to move up in their careers or get a promotion, resulting in less motivated employees.

Workers are paid for their skills and jobs, and as skills and job descriptions vary, so does the salary bracket. The drawback of the broadband pay structure is that multiple job positions are paid similarly, which is unfair as some employees have to work harder, with a higher skill set compared to others.

(47) (D) All of the above.

Effective strategic planning can boost productivity, reduce turnover rate, increase proficiency, strengthen customer relationships with the company and increase profits. Employee engagement is a crucial factor that benefits a company greatly.

(48) (D) Not helping employees with difficult tasks.

Employee engagement is usually a lacking factor in most businesses. The employees occasionally need guidance with tasks not within their expertise or with generally difficult projects. There are many different ways in which employees can be engaged with their company.

Conducting surveys annually and monthly, keeping track of all engagement activity and preparing the employees for their work with proper instructions and resources are just a few ways to increase employee engagement.

(49) (A) Promote communication and encourage employees to give feedback.

Feedback plays an important role in engaging employees with their work. The employees are free to comment on what resources the company lacks, what needs to improve, etc.

Similarly, when employees receive feedback from their supervisors and managers, they tend to improve weak areas in their performance.

(50) (D) All of the above.

Employee engagement is defined as the connection the employees feel with their company. Their devotion to their work and the effort they put into their jobs is also known as employee engagement.

(51) (B) Employee engagement.

Employee engagement is defined as the connection employees feel with their company. Conducting surveys annually and monthly, keeping track of all engagement activity and preparing the employees for their work with proper instructions and resources are just a few ways to increase employee engagement.

(52) (B) Making employees feel valued.

The ability of an organization to keep its employees is known as employee retention. It requires making employees feel valued.

(53) (A) HR.

HR is responsible for any factors related to employees, so employee engagement is also their responsibility.

(54) (C) Conducting surveys and interviews.

Conducting surveys annually and monthly, keeping track of all engagement activity and preparing the employees for their work with proper instructions and resources are just a few ways HR can measure employee engagement.

(55) (C) Unstructured.

Unstructured interviews are characterized by open-ended questions about a candidate's background, work experience, interests, skills, and motivations. While other interview types may also cover past work experience, they have more specific definitions that don't necessarily focus on previous experience as the primary topic.

(56) (C) Structured.

Structured interviews are interviews with a set number of questions. All employees are asked the same questions. These questions are predefined so all or most parties are aware of the questions.

(57) (B) Work/life balance.

The balance between working hours and leisure time is known as work/life balance. Jack makes sure he has enough time for his family and his work, so the term work-life balance best fits his situation.

(58) (C) Negligence and noncompliance.

Neglecting work and not providing work on time is not a workplace policy. Employees must complete all work accordingly and on time.

(59) (A) Alternative work arrangements.

Alternative work arrangements are different types of work conditions that an organization may provide. These include remote working, telecommuting and flexible work. These arrangements are made so the employees can work according to their needs and their conditions.

(60) (A) Condensed work.

Condensed work or a condensed workweek is an alternative work arrangement in which the employees work more daily hours, not the typical nine to five. In return, they get an extended weekend of three days.

(61) (D) Shift.

Working for specific hours in either the day or the night is known as shift work. This type of work ultimately benefits employers as work continues throughout the day and night.

(62) (B) Flextime.

A work arrangement in which the employees are free to work according to their availability is called flextime. The employees are only required to send in their work on time.

(63) (C) Hybrid.

A workplace where both on-site and off-site workers are working is known as hybrid work. The workers are selected for a specific type of work based on their requirements and working conditions.

(64) (B) He is setting boundaries.

Some ways in which employees or their company can set boundaries include prohibiting workers from entering a workplace after specific hours, not responding to calls during vacations or after office hours, and not responding to work emails or calls outside the office.

(65) (D) Allotting all employees free time every second week, ensuring they adhere to it.

Implementing an employee engagement plan is the same as implementing a strategic plan. Certain steps need to be followed, such as handling finances, appointing team leaders, taking surveys and giving feedback.

(66) (A) Family-friendly policies.

Many companies set family-friendly policies that help employees with their work-life balance. These include day care at the office and celebrating days such as bring your child to work day.

(67) (D) All of the above.

Although customer satisfaction and good financial aspects are important factors that boost a company's success, employee engagement is also considered a crucial driver of this.

(68) (C) Disrespect employees and their boundaries.

Disrespecting employees and their boundaries can increase employee dissatisfaction and decrease time-to-productivity, leading to delays and disengagement.

(69) (B) The Employee Polygraph Protection Act.

The Employee Polygraph Protection Act states that most private businesses are prohibited from conducting lie detector tests for pre-employment screening or during employment. This statute makes it illegal for companies to discriminate against employees who decline such examinations.

The federal government, on the other hand, has the authority to administer lie detector tests to persons engaged in national security–related activities. Private businesses can also conduct polygraph testing if a workplace event results in financial damage.

(70) (A) Wage disparity based on gender.

The Equal Pay Act sought to eliminate salary disparities between the sexes and pay discrimination based on gender. It was signed by John F. Kennedy and is an amendment to the Fair Labor Standard Act.

Regardless of gender, the EPA protects all persons equally. All types of remuneration, including bonuses, salary, insurance, paid holidays and other perks, are included.

(71) (B) The Fair and Accurate Credit Transactions Act.

The Fair and Accurate Credit Transactions Act (FACT) is an amendment to the Fair Credit Reporting Act (FRCA) that includes requirements to improve the accuracy of credit-related information for consumers. Once a year, it permits customers to acquire a free copy of their credit information from reporting agencies.

FRCA is another federal legislation governing credit information collection and credit reports from consumers. It was enacted to address information accuracy, fairness and privacy in the national credit reporting bureaus' files.

(72) (C) The IRS Intermediate Sanctions (2002).

The IRS can impose intermediate fines on an individual involved in an unreasonably beneficial transaction. A nonprofit organization pays more or receives less than fair market value in this kind of transaction. The most prevalent type of excess benefit transaction includes excessive payment for services.

(73) (A) To prohibit employers from interfering with employees' rights to organize into trade unions and engage in bargaining and strikes.

The fundamental goal of the National Labor Relations Act of 1935 is to safeguard employees' rights, encourage collective bargaining and regulate private-sector labor and management activities that might harm workers or the economy.

This statute also prohibits employers from interfering with employees organizing, forming or assisting a labor organization or from working together to improve the conditions of employment.

(74) (C) Layoffs exceeding six months.

The Worker Adjustment and Retraining Notification Act (1988) covers employment losses like terminations, layoffs exceeding six months and more than 50% reductions in employees' work hours each month of any six months.

(75) (A) Federal employees to organize, bargain collectively and participate in labor organizations.

The Civil Service Reform Act of 1978 granted federal employees the right to organize, negotiate collectively and join labor unions. It also outlined most government employees' performance and assessment systems, disciplinary procedures and appeals processes.

The goal of the bill was to provide federal managers the freedom they needed to enhance government operations and productivity while safeguarding employees from unfair practices.

(76) (A) Union members can be employed in a closed shop, while non-union members must pay union dues in an agency shop.

A closed shop is a workplace where only union members are allowed to work, and the union has strong negotiating leverage since it can regulate who is recruited.

On the other hand, an agency shop arrangement is a workplace in which non-union members must pay union dues but are not forced to join the union. This is because non-union members profit from collective bargaining and other union operations, and it is only right that they participate financially.

(77) (A) Reduces, increases.

Employee engagement and unionization have a complicated and multidirectional relationship, although strong employee involvement can reduce the risk of unionization. This is because employees who are happy with their jobs and workplaces are less likely to want to organize a union.

On the other hand, unionization can increase employee engagement since unionized employees have more authority and a voice in the workplace and are thus more likely to feel involved in their work and workplace. As a result, option A is the correct answer.

(78) (D) Making initial contact.

The initial step in the union campaign and election process is to contact employees interested in union representation. It is normally accomplished through informational sessions or one-on-one conversations with potential personnel.

(79) (B) Peaceful protests.

Peaceful protests, no violence or intimidation, respect for property rights, fair treatment of replacement employees and compliance with labor regulations are among the essential strike criteria.

Protesting peacefully entails marching and demonstrating outside the workplace. The other answer options are collective bargaining principles rather than striking rules.

(80) (D) Listen to the employee.

It is important to fully understand the employee's perspective and gather all necessary information before making decisions.

(81) (B) Investigate.

HR should always investigate the situation if a grievance involves an alleged violation of company policies. This involves interviewing witnesses, reviewing documents and conducting relevant research.

(82) (B) Accidents and injuries.

A safe workplace can reduce the risk of accidents and injuries in the workplace. It also increases employee trust and satisfaction with the organization. A safe workplace can improve a business's position and market reputation.

(83) (B) Working in and implementing a safety culture within the organization.

The responsibility of the top management is to ensure employees are working in and reinforcing a culture of safety within the organization. A safety culture increases employee trust and loyalty, improves OSHA compliance and enables organizations to recruit top talent.

(84) (C) Report any safety concerns or hazards they encounter.

New policies flow from the top down, and supervisors play a key role in preventing accidents in the workplace. So, they should be aware of workplace safety regulations implemented by OSHA, as well as procedures.

Supervisors should monitor employees to ensure they operate safely and adhere to established safety measures. This involves looking for risky practices in employees and detecting possible dangers.

Moreover, employees should be encouraged to report any safety problems or risks they notice since this can assist in preventing accidents and workplace injuries.

(85) (C) Performing a risk assessment.

The first step in safeguarding a workplace is to identify the present risks. This may be accomplished through a risk assessment considering criteria such as the type of business, location and history of crime in the region.

(86) (C) Promoting good hygiene.

Employers may aid in the prevention of infectious disease transmission by encouraging proper hygiene, providing hand sanitizer and other hygiene products and promoting vaccination.

Employee assistance programs are linked to avoiding substance abuse. In contrast, ergonomic workstations and restricting the time employees spend performing repetitive activities are related to preventing repetitive motion disorders, which are two separate concerns.

(87) (A) Alter its fundamental elements, including its practices, culture, workforce, offerings, infrastructure and technological advancements.

The acts of a firm to modify its core features, such as its procedures, culture, employees, offers, infrastructure and technological advancements, are referred to as organizational change.

(88) (B) Proactive planning.

Business continuity management is the proactive planning and preparation to ensure that an organization's critical business functions can be carried out in an emergency.

(89) (A) Unifies its various technical models to ensure they align and sync with the corporate culture.

When a firm combines its multiple technological models to ensure they sync with the corporate culture, it is called business integration. Business integration facilitates communication flows, company culture and technological integration goals.

(90) (A) The spouses and children (under 21) of treaty traders, treaty investors or employees of enterprises.

The spouses and children (under 21) of treaty traders, treaty investors or employees of enterprises are allowed to receive a dependent E visa. However, they may not have the same nationality as the applicant.

Test 3: Questions

(1) What are HR strategies?

(A) Pulling workers aside daily for feedback

(B) Plans to manage employees and accomplish objectives

(C) Brainstorming ideas to help create an inclusive workplace culture

(D) Both (B) and (C)

(2) Which of the following is true for HR strategies?

(A) They may be classified into two types.

(B) They concentrate on company practices.

(C) They ensure a company can attract and retain the maximum number of employees.

(D) They just concentrate on employee needs.

(3) Which of the following best describes the full-time vs. part-time employee classification?

(A) It is determined by the number of hours an employee works per week.

(B) It is driven by the conditions of the employee's contract.

(C) It is dependent on the duration of the work.

(D) It is dependent on whether the worker is paid full time or part time.

(4) Why do companies categorize their employees?

(A) To have them in groups depending on their expertise and skills

(B) To make compensation-related decisions

(C) To regularly analyze and update their systems

(D) All of the above

(5) The HR department is essential to achieving an organization's goals and objectives by ____________.

(A) Hiring, training and managing employees

(B) Managing, engaging and keeping workers

(C) Coordinating, organizing and assigning employees

(D) Recruiting, keeping and growing employees

(6) HR compliance involves ____________.

(A) Making performance requirements, performing evaluations and giving feedback to staff

(B) Overseeing the preparation and administering of the organization's compensation and benefits programs

(C) Ensuring agreement with all applicable employment regulations, such as labor laws and anti-discrimination legislation

(D) Overseeing attracting, recruiting and selecting new personnel because of the business

(7) Which of the following must be viewed when choosing a work screening tool?

(A) Validity

(B) Job analysis

(C) Cost

(D) Both (A) and (C)

(8) What is the goal of any credit check?

(A) It verifies the candidate's previous job and employment history titles, duties and dates of employment.

(B) It confirms the applicant has the educational qualifications claimed on the résumé.

(C) It verifies the candidate's credit history and financial stability.

(D) It verifies the candidate has no criminal history or record of severe offenses.

(9) What is "license verification?"

(A) It is a method that verifies the applicant has no criminal history or record of severe offenses.

(B) It is a method that verifies the candidate's previous employment history, duties and dates of employment.

(C) It is a process that confirms the candidate has the necessary licenses or certifications required for the job.

(D) It is a method that confirms the applicant has the educational qualifications reported on the résumé.

(10) What is substance abuse screening?

(A) It is a process that tests job applicants or employees for drugs or alcohol in their system.

(B) It is a method that tests candidates' abilities and skills for the job.

(C) It is a method that requires testing to assess an applicant's potential to process information and make specific choices.

(D) None of the above.

(11) Which of the following best describes active listening?

(A) Listening but not paying enough attention

(B) Giving the candidate your complete attention and being present in the moment

(C) Being constantly distracted while listening

(D) Mentally preparing for what you'll say coming

(12) Why should HR professionals be conscious of nonverbal communication cues?

(A) To offer invaluable information about the persona of the candidate

(B) To get much better at communicating

(C) To socialize

(D) None of the above

(13) Which interview assesses a candidate's past experiences and attitudes?

(A) Structured interview

(B) Unstructured interview

(C) Mock interview

(D) Behavioral assessment

(14) In a competency-based interview, an interviewer will _________.

(A) Use active listening

(B) Follow a predetermined range of concerns

(C) Focus on the capability of the person to perform certain tasks

(D) Perform an intelligence questionnaire

(15) Which of the following isn't true of a case study interview?

(A) It provides applicants with a real-life business scenario and asks them to find an answer.

(B) It analyzes the decision-making abilities of the interviewer.

(C) It evaluates candidates on the basis of their replies.

(D) It analyzes the problem-solving skills of a prospect.

(16) An HR manager is able to avoid candidate-order errors and pressure-to-hire by _______________.

(A) Comparing each applicant with the prior one

(B) Making choices based on relative performance over complete performance

(C) Taking frequent pauses and evaluating applicants based on worthiness

(D) Employing a structured interview approach

(17) What is considered an internal element of how a company deals with its employees?

(A) Competition

(B) Management style

(C) Rules

(D) Technological improvements

(18) A business is implementing a new training program for its employees. The HR division decides to conduct pre- and post-examinations.

What is the goal of pre- and post-assessments in this situation?

(A) To find personnel who need training

(B) To evaluate the ability of people before and after instruction

(C) To figure out the quality of educational materials

(D) To understand the duration of the instructional program

(19) What are learning curves?

(A) Methods for calculating employee productivity

(B) Techniques for evaluating the effectiveness of training

(C) A type of instruction program

(D) Diagrams of the relationship between the skill of individuals performing a job and their experience

(20) What is the aim of learning curves?

(A) To evaluate employee satisfaction

(B) To track training progress and predict performance

(C) To build employee compensation

(D) To determine employee turnover rates

(21) What are the four kinds of learning curves?

(A) Diminishing, increasing, decreasing and complex

(B) Simple, complex, exponential and linear

(C) Increasing, decreasing, stagnant and irregular

(D) Diminishing, descending, rising and stagnant

(22) What is in-house training?

(A) Training provided by internal employees

(B) Training provided by external consultants

(C) Training given by federal agencies

(D) Training given by universities

(23) What are the steps required in developing a training program?

(A) Define the training goals, evaluate staff needs, decide on the delivery technique, develop the content, pick a teacher, schedule the training, assess the effectiveness and keep track of progress

(B) Define the training goals, create the articles, choose a professor, schedule the training as well as evaluate the effectiveness

(C) Define the training goals, assess employee needs, figure out the delivery method as well as create the content

(D) Define the training goals, assess employee needs, figure out the delivery method and evaluate effectiveness

(24) What is the purpose of evaluating a training program?

(A) To determine opportunities for development and find out if the coaching plan has attained its objectives and goals

(B) To establish employee turnover rates

(C) To build employee compensation

(D) To measure employee satisfaction

(25) What are a few techniques for evaluating training?

(A) Classroom teaching and online courses

(B) In-house training

(C) Evaluations, observations, surveys and responses, performance evaluations, together with ROI analysis

(D) Evaluations, surveys and employee interviews

(26) What is the time sequence design technique for computing training effectiveness?

(A) A mathematical analysis that examines the consequences of the course on the students prior to and after the instruction

(B) An approach to evaluating education based on participant feedback

(C) An approach to analyzing education based on employee turnover rates

(D) An approach to analyzing education based on employee job performance

(27) What are post-training and pre-assessments utilized for?

(A) To determine the knowledge and abilities the participant had before and after the training program

(B) To collect responses from participants through surveys and one-on-one meetings

(C) To determine the financial advantages of the training program

(D) To determine the outcomes of the instruction on the students prior to and after the instruction

(28) What is the increasing learning curve?

(A) The pace of advancement is sluggish at first; however, it slowly increases until complete proficiency is attained.

(B) The speed of progression increases quickly in the beginning but decreases over time.

(C) The speed of learning is sluggish in the beginning, and the learner becomes proficient later on.

(D) The beginning of the curve shows gradual learning; the curve exhibits an increase later on.

(29) What is outside training?

(A) Training completed by federal agencies

(B) Training completed by mentors that work for the same company

(C) Training completed by universities

(D) Training performed by an individual not from the business

(30) What is the objective of checking improvement in a training course?

(A) To make sure employees are maintaining the abilities and knowledge they have acquired

(B) To assess employee turnover rates

(C) To establish employee compensation

(D) To evaluate the monetary advantages of the training program

(31) What is the diminishing learning curve?

(A) The speed of progress goes up quickly at the start but then decreases as time passes.

(B) The speed of progress is sluggish in the beginning; however, it slowly increases until total proficiency is achieved.

(C) Both (A) and (B)

(D) None of the above

(32) What is the complicated learning curve?

(A) It shows a brand-new learner as the learning is sluggish in the beginning, and later on, the learner becomes adept and requires a shorter time to do the task.

(B) The speed of progress is sluggish in the beginning; however, it slowly increases until total proficiency is achieved.

(C) The starting point of the curve demonstrates slow learning, and afterward, the curve exhibits a rise, suggesting the learner is getting better at carrying out the job.

(D) The speed of development increases quickly in the beginning but subsequently decreases over time, signaling the trainee has gotten to his or her limit or perhaps is not motivated any longer.

(33) A building company hired a subcontractor to carry out the power work on a venture. According to the Davis-Bacon Act, which of the following is correct?

(A) Since the subcontractor isn't the primary contractor, they don't need to pay the workers at the market rate.

(B) Because the project is covered by the Davis-Bacon Act, the subcontractor must pay workers the current wage.

(C) The subcontractor must spend prevailing wages only on electricians.

(D) The Davis Bacon Act does not affect the subcontractor because they do electric work.

(34) The employees at a company are part of a union. The union produces a new collective bargaining agreement that raises each employee's pay.

How will this influence the way the business decides to pay its personnel?

(A) The company will have to give all unionized employees a pay raise.

(B) The business will non-unionize pay for employees.

(C) The business will ignore the pay raise for unionized employees and risk a strike.

(D) The business will speak with the union about a smaller pay raise.

(35) An individual will work in another country for two years. The employee will work on a project expected to bring in a lot of money for the business.

What kind of pay should the company give the employee working abroad?

(A) The same pay as the worker in their home country

(B) The same pay as the local workers in the foreign country

(C) A higher salary with bonuses or profit-sharing opportunities based on how well the project goes

(D) No extra pay because the worker is already being given a chance to work abroad

(36) An employee has always met or outperformed performance goals for the past six months.

What is the best way to reward her and let her know how well she did?

(A) A promotion

(B) A personalized thank-you note from the boss

(C) A cash bonus or a raise

(D) A small gift card to a local restaurant or store

(37) Which debts or legal responsibilities may result in a wage garnishment?

(A) Union dues, medical expenses and auto loans

(B) Credit card, mortgage and student loan debt

(C) Child support payments, tax debts and unpaid court fines

(D) Gym memberships, subscription services and personal loans

(38) What is the Age Discrimination in Employment Act?

(A) A federal law that forbids discrimination against 40-year-old or older employees/job applicants

(B) A state law restricting employers from discrimination against workers or maybe business individuals on the foundation of gender or race

(C) A federal law that requires minimum wage and overtime pay for workers

(D) A state law requiring the granting of medical leave and family leave to qualified personnel

(39) What is the ranking technique in job evaluation?

(A) A method that compares job opportunities to a regular job

(B) A means of assessing occupations based on their required knowledge, abilities and capabilities

(C) A technique that ranks jobs based on their relevance or significance in the business

(D) A procedure by which workers are evaluated based on their influence on the business's economic success

(40) A fashion retailer would like to create a competitive compensation program to entice and keep staff.

What is the first action the business must take?

(A) Conduct a business pay practices poll.

(B) Establish salary ranges for each work.

(C) Establish a salary structure.

(D) Pick a benchmark to develop consistency.

(41) A company wants to reward its sales staff for up-selling additional products to customers.

Which incentive is most likely to accomplish this objective?

(A) A paid vacation for the sales staff at a neighboring resort

(B) A financial reward for promoting a particular number of items to each consumer

(C) An email sent to the entire organization announcing the salesperson who sold the most things

(D) A company automobile for the best salesperson

(42) How often should incentives be provided to teams?

(A) Once every month

(B) Each trimester

(C) Annually

(D) Depends on the outcomes sought

(43) A major characteristic of any Scanlon plan is __________.

(A) Employment assurance for most employees

(B) A profit-sharing program that compensates employees based on the performance of the company

(C) A compensation process that ensures equal remuneration for equal work

(D) A technique for settling employee complaints

(44) Company XYZ allows its employees to work from home two days a week. What type of non-cash reward will the company offer its workers?

(A) Health insurance

(B) Paid vacation time

(C) Flexible work arrangements

(D) Stock options

(45) What is a commission plan?

(A) A strategy providing salespeople with the same amount of cash for every purchase they make

(B) A strategy providing salespeople with a share of the benefit from every purchase they generate

(C) A strategy that gives salespeople a percentage of their total sales

(D) All of the above

(46) What is an at-risk pay plan?

(A) A strategy that pays workers based on how long they've been with the business

(B) A strategy that gives employees the required amount of cash for each hour they work

(C) A strategy that offers employees the same amount of annual salary

(D) A strategy that provides employees a percentage of their salary based on how well they do their tasks

(47) Which of the following are crucial ingredients of HRM?

(A) Discovering what workers require

(B) Ensuring performance appraisal and control

(C) Discouraging personnel management

(D) Distributing financial aspects

(48) A systematic analysis is required by a performance appraisal to _______.

(A) Ensure employees complete work on time

(B) Make sure employees meet and exceed performance expectations

(C) Identify improvement areas

(D) Both (B) and (C)

(49) Which of the following best describes a performance appraisal?

(A) A process of evaluating an employee's performance against set goals or criteria

(B) A tool for identifying employee training and development needs

(C) A process for making reward and recognition-based decisions

(D) All of the above

(50) A performance appraisal involves ________.

(A) Skill assessments

(B) Performance objectives

(C) Employee contribution to the organization

(D) All of the above

(51) After a performance appraisal, the feedback given to the employees helps them identify ____________.

(A) Areas of improvement

(B) Time management issues

(C) What they did well

(D) None of the above

(52) ________ can conduct a performance appraisal.

(A) Managers

(B) Supervisors

(C) Stakeholders

(D) All of the above

(53) The purpose of a performance appraisal is to __________.

(A) Identify customer needs

(B) Evaluate the employees' skills

(C) Provide feedback on employees' performance

(D) Appreciate employees

(54) The performance appraisal process needs to be based on _________.

(A) The organization's needs

(B) Customer service

(C) A clear and objective set of criteria

(D) Fair and vague objectives

(55) Which of the following helps eliminate bias and ensures a fair and objective appraisal?

(A) Standardized evaluation tools

(B) Strict measures toward employees

(C) Keeping track of customer service

(D) Making fair judgments

(56) The performance appraisal is conducted ___________.

(A) Monthly

(B) Annually or semiannually

(C) Weekly

(D) Once in two years

(57) What is not a step in the performance appraisal process?

(A) Planning and goal setting

(B) Appraisal preparation

(C) Review and follow-up

(D) Defining the company's vision

(58) HR managers discuss ten employees' performance over the year. Which of the following best describes this situation?

(A) Appraisal meeting

(B) Performance documentation

(C) Review and follow-up

(D) Ongoing feedback

(59) A manager provides comments on the current work of an employee. Which of the following best describes this situation?

(A) Appraisal meeting

(B) Performance documentation

(C) Review and follow-up

(D) Ongoing feedback

(60) Keeping a record of the employees' performance in meetings, emails and work is known as a/an:

(A) Appraisal meeting

(B) Performance documentation

(C) Review and follow-up

(D) Ongoing feedback

(61) A review of the documented performance of the employees is drawn up during __________.

(A) An appraisal meeting

(B) Performance documentation

(C) Review and follow-up

(D) Ongoing feedback

(62) Which of the following is an important purpose of performance documentation in the context of human resources?

(A) Evaluating employee eligibility for promotions.

(B) Establishing a formal reprimand process.

(C) Determining employee vacation entitlement.

(D) Tracking employee attendance records.

(63) The primary goal of customized talent management is _________.

(A) Recruiting top talent

(B) Recruiting average employees

(C) Appointing managers for multiple teams

(D) Firing unneeded employees

(64) A recruiter finds a candidate charismatic and hires him instead of other candidates.

Which of the following best describes this case?

(A) Rating error

(B) Halo effect

(C) Central tendency bias

(D) Unfair judgment

(65) Which of the following prohibits discrimination based on race, gender and sex?

(A) The Civil Rights Act of 1964

(B) The Americans with Disability Act

(C) The Fair Labor Standards Act

(D) The Age Discrimination in Employment Act

(66) If an employee acts defensively during an appraisal interview, the manager should ___________.

(A) Chastise the employee.

(B) Be empathetic and understanding.

(C) Provide feedback that further decreases employee morale.

(D) Blame the employee for the problem.

(67) A performance appraisal is an important part of _______.

(A) Total quality management

(B) Customized talent management

(C) HR management

(D) Performance evaluation

(68) A marketer chooses to grade the scores of all of the applicants as normal. This is an example of a/an __________.

(A) Rating mistake

(B) Halo effect

(C) Central tendency bias

(D) Unfair judgment

(69) Which law regulates credit reports?

(A) The Fair and Accurate Credit Transactions Act

(B) The Equal Credit Opportunity Act

(C) The Fair Reporting Credit Act

(D) The Fair Debt Collection Practices Act

(70) Which law prohibits the use of lie detector tests for pre-employment screening or during employment?

(A) The Employee Polygraph Protection Act

(B) The Equal Pay Act

(C) The Fair Labor Standards Act

(D) The Health Insurance and Portability and Accountability Act

(71) Which law was passed to promote financial stability and protect consumers from abusive financial deals?

(A) The Copeland "Anti-kickback" Act

(B) The Davis-Bacon Act

(C) The Dodd-Frank Wall Street Reform and Consumer Protection Act

(D) The Economic Growth and Tax Relief Reconciliation Act

(72) Which law prohibits discrimination based on disability in federal government programs and federal contractors' employment practices?

(A) The Immigration Reform and Control Act of 1986

(B) The Rehabilitation Act (1973)

(C) The Retirement Equity Act

(D) The Social Security Act (1935)

(73) What is the role of top management in safety?

(A) To create and implement a safety culture within the organization

(B) To ensure employees are adequately trained to recognize and respond to potential hazards

(C) To regularly review and assess the effectiveness of the organization's safety program

(D) All of the above

(74) Which act provides for minimum wage and fringe benefits, as well as other conditions of work under service contracts?

(A) The Immigration and Nationality Act of 1952

(B) The Pension Protection Act of 2006

(C) The Service Contract Act of 1965

(D) The Small Business Job Protection Act of 1996

(75) Which of the following refers to the negotiation process between an employer and a union representing its employees?

(A) Labor relations

(B) Unionization

(C) Collective bargaining

(D) Employee engagement

(76) What are some examples of unsafe conditions that can cause accidents in the workplace?

(A) Improperly guarded equipment

(B) Defective equipment

(C) Hazardous procedures around machines

(D) All of the above

(77) What is OSHA's role in workplace safety?

(A) OSHA makes guidelines for workplace safety and implements them.

(B) OSHA trains employees on safety protocols.

(C) OSHA conducts inspections of workplaces to ensure employers comply with safety standards.

(D) None of the above.

(78) What is collective bargaining?

(A) A process in which representatives of employees and employers negotiate the employment terms and conditions of employment.

(B) An arrangement in which non-union members are required to pay union dues but are not required to join the union.

(C) A workplace in which only union members are allowed to be employed.

(D) An act that limits the ability of courts to issue injunctions against unions and employees in labor disputes.

(79) Why is creating a secure workplace crucial for an organization?

(A) It fosters a sense of trust between management and employees.

(B) It lowers workers' compensation costs.

(C) It raises an organization's brand reputation.

(D) All of the above.

(80) What is the intent behind the union drive and election process?

(A) To enhance working conditions for union members

(B) To determine whether the employees would like to be represented by a union

(C) To participate in collective bargaining with employers

(D) To build a union shop agreement in the workplace

(81) What is the supervisor's role in accident prevention?

(A) Knowing about security policies and procedures in the office

(B) Monitoring staff to make sure they follow established security protocols

(C) Encouraging staff to report safety concerns

(D) All of the above

(82) Which of the following laws guarantees the right of employees to engage in collective bargaining and protects employees against retaliation for union activities?

(A) The Taft-Hartley Act

(B) The National Labor Relations Act

(C) The Norris-LaGuardia Act

(D) The Wagner Act

(83) How can employers limit workplace accidents?

(A) By reducing unsafe conditions in the workplace

(B) By providing proper training to employees on how to operate equipment safely

(C) By implementing safety protocols for hazardous work procedures

(D) All of the above

(84) Which act outlawed yellow-dog contracts in which employees agree not to participate in any labor union?

(A) The Labor Management Relations Act of 1947

(B) The National Labor Relations Act of 1935

(C) The Norris-LaGuardia Act

(D) The Occupational Safety and Health Act of 1970

(85) What is organizational change?

(A) The actions of a company to alter its basic elements

(B) A company's decision to reduce its workforce

(C) A company's financial performance

(D) A company's marketing strategy

(86) What is the purpose of a change management strategy?

(A) To increase revenue

(B) To avoid undesirable consequences such as a company interruption and subsequent lost productivity

(C) To reduce the number of employees

(D) To implement hasty changes

(87) What is business continuity management?

(A) A reactive plan for emergencies

(B) A hands-on plan that ensures that a company can meet its important business duties in the event of an urgent situation

(C) A plan to reduce the number of employees

(D) A plan to increase revenues

(88) What is HR's role in ensuring business continuity?

(A) Creating and putting into practice business continuity strategies

(B) Providing guidelines and practices for workers' behavior when a disturbance occurs

(C) Giving employees disaster preparedness training

(D) All of the above

(89) Why are mergers and acquisitions successful?

(A) They require large-scale organizational change.

(B) They involve prompt and secure data integration.

(C) They allow companies to create enormous value.

(D) All of the above.

(90) What is the role of data integration in a successful merger or acquisition?

(A) It is not important to the success of mergers and acquisitions.

(B) It is only important for financial services organizations.

(C) It is a crucial component for the prompt and secure integration of data.

(D) It is only important for companies in the technology industry.

Test 3: Answers & Explanations

(1) (B) Plans to manage employees and accomplish objectives.

HR strategies are plans and methods used by companies to manage their employees and accomplish their objectives.

(2) (C) They ensure a company can attract and retain the maximum number of employees.

A company's most pressing problems can be resolved with the help of an HR strategy. It enhances the importance of hiring, talent management, remuneration, succession planning and corporate culture and necessitates HR input during policy formation.

With this approach, a company can attract and retain top employees. An HR strategy can be classified into corporate, competitive and functional.

(3) (A) It is determined by the number of hours an employee works per week.

Full-time employment is typically defined as working 30 to 40 hours per week, and part-time work is typically defined as working less than 30 hours per week. Therefore, it is determined by the number of hours worked.

(4) (B) To make compensation-related decisions.

With employee categorization, employers can pay employees per their positions' obligations, challenges and complexity. They can make valuable decisions such as salaries, benefits and promotions.

(5) (D) Recruiting, keeping and growing employees.

The HR department is crucial to achieving the organization's goals and objectives by recruiting, retaining and growing qualified staff.

(6) (C) Ensuring agreement with all applicable employment regulations, such as labor laws and antidiscrimination legislation.

HR compliance refers to abiding by all relevant labor laws and legislation.

(7) (D) Both (A) and (C).

Some considerations when selecting a job screening tool involve job recruitment, legal considerations, validity and reliability, cost and time, objectivity, ease of use and customization.

(8) (C) It verifies the candidate's credit history and financial stability.

A credit check is one of the elements involved in a candidate's background investigation.

(9) (C) It is a process that confirms the candidate has the necessary licenses or certifications required for the job.

License verification is one of the elements involved in background checking.

(10) (A) It is a process that tests job applicants or employees for drugs or alcohol in their system.

Substance abuse screening tests job applicants or employees for the presence of drugs or alcohol in their system. It aims to determine if a candidate or employee is fit for duty and able to perform the essential functions of the job safely and effectively.

(11) (B) Giving the candidate your complete attention and being present in the moment.

This involves giving the candidate your full attention and being present in the moment instead of thinking about your next question or mentally preparing for what you will say next.

(12) (A) To offer invaluable information about the persona of the candidate.

HR personnel must be conscious of nonverbal communication cues, like body language and tone of voice, since they can give invaluable insights into the candidate's character and suitability for the job.

(13) (D) Behavioral assessment.

Behavioral interviewing entails asking potential applicants about their previous experiences. The interviewer asks about particular circumstances and experiences and seeks examples of the way the candidate has shown specific skills.

(14) (C) Focus on the capability of the person to perform certain tasks.

A competency-based interview evaluates the person's abilities and capabilities required for the project.

(15) (C) It evaluates candidates on the basis of their replies.

In a case study interview, the individual is provided with a real business situation and then required to give solutions. This enables the interviewer to assess the applicant's problem-solving, analytical and decision-making abilities.

(16) (C) Taking frequent pauses and evaluating applicants based on worthiness.

Interviewing a number of candidates sequentially can result in what's referred to as the candidate-order mistake. This happens when the interviewer compares the next person to the prior candidate and makes a decision based on the comparison instead of performance.

To avoid these errors, it's essential for interviewers to take frequent pauses and assess each applicant on their worth.

(17) (B) Management style.

You will find internal and external variables that could impact the leadership style of the HR department. Internal variables include company structure, management style, staff demographics and company building.

External variables include monetary factors, competition, regulatory environment and technical developments.

(18) (B) To evaluate the ability of people before and after instruction.

The objective of carrying out pre- and post-assessments in this particular situation would be to evaluate the usefulness of the training course by looking at the functionality of staff members prior to and after the instruction.

This lets HR discover if the training plan was effective in enhancing employee performance and achieving the company's objectives.

(19) (D) Diagrams of the relationship between the skill of individuals performing a job and their experience.

Learning curves are diagrams of the relationship between the skill of individuals doing a job and how much experience they have.

Because individuals acquire more experience carrying out a job, their competence or performance usually gets better, so the learning curve symbolizes this particular connection.

(20) (B) To track training progress and predict performance.

The purpose of learning curves is to track training progress and predict performance. Learning curves can help trainers and managers understand how long it will take learners to achieve proficiency in a new skill or task.

They can also help identify where learners may struggle in the learning process.

(21) (D) Diminishing, descending, rising and stagnant.

The four kinds of learning curves are decreasing, increasing, descending and stagnant.

The decreasing learning curve indicates a fast improvement in performance in the beginning, followed by a slow improvement rate as the job gets harder.

The rising learning curve indicates a gradual improvement as time passes. In comparison, the decreasing learning curve refers to dwindling effectiveness over time, while the stagnant learning curve sees absolutely no improvement in performance in the long run.

(22) (A) Training provided by internal employees.

In-house instruction is training provided by coaches that work for the same organization. This kind of instruction could be personalized to match the business's unique requirements and might be much more cost-effective than external training.

(23) (A) Define the training goals, evaluate staff needs, decide on the delivery technique, develop the content, pick a teacher, schedule the training, assess the effectiveness and keep track of progress.

These measures make sure that the training course fulfills the requirements of both the group and the students.

(24) (A) To determine opportunities for development and find out if the coaching plan has attained its objectives and goals.

The objective of analyzing a training course is usually to recognize improvement places and find out whether it has met its goals and objectives. Evaluation enables instructors and supervisors to determine the weaknesses and strengths of the training plan and make needed improvements.

(25) (C) Evaluations, observations, surveys and responses, performance evaluations, together with ROI analysis.

A number of techniques for assessing training include pre- and post-training evaluations, observations, feedback and surveys, performance assessments and ROI analysis.

These techniques can assist teachers and administrators in assessing the training program's success and figuring out improvement areas.

(26) (A) A mathematical analysis that examines the consequences of the course on the students prior to and after the instruction.

The time sequence design technique of determining training success is a method of statistical analysis that analyzes the consequences of the instruction on the students prior to and after the instruction.

This method helps instructors and supervisors figure out the effect of the instruction on learner performance.

(27) (D) To determine the outcomes of the instruction on the students prior to and after the instruction.

Pre- and post-training examinations are employed to assess the consequences of the instruction on the learners prior to and after the instruction. This technique allows instructors and administrators to figure out how much students have learned.

(28) (A) The pace of advancement is sluggish at first; however, it slowly increases until complete proficiency is attained.

The increasing learning curve signifies slow learning in the beginning, followed by a steady rise in proficiency until complete proficiency is attained. This kind of learning curve is typical for complicated assignments or abilities.

(29) (D) Training performed by an individual not from the business.

External training is completed by somebody, not for the company. This particular kind of instruction could be handy when the business doesn't have the needed in-house knowledge or when the instructor is extremely skilled.

(30) (A) To make sure employees are maintaining the abilities and knowledge they have acquired.

The objective of checking improvement in a training plan is usually to make sure that workers keep the abilities and knowledge they've obtained.

(31) (A) The speed of progress goes up quickly at the start but then decreases as time passes.

The decreasing learning curve indicates a fast improvement in performance in the beginning, followed by a slow rate of development as the job gets harder. This kind of learning curve is typical for complicated jobs calling for practice and effort to perfect.

(32) (C) The starting point of the curve demonstrates slow learning, and afterward, the curve exhibits a rise, suggesting the learner is getting better at carrying out the job.

The complicated learning curve signifies slow learning initially, followed by a progressive improvement in proficiency until complete proficiency is attained.

This particular learning curve can include times of regression or plateaus in effectiveness, which indicates that the learning procedure is a lot more complex compared to some other learning curves.

(33) (B) Because the project is covered by the Davis-Bacon Act, the subcontractor must pay workers the current wage.

The Davis-Bacon Act is a federal law that mandates contractors and subcontractors to pay workers on federally funded construction projects prevailing rates and benefits.

Under this act, the workers must be paid fairly according to the market rates of the job, or legal action can be taken against the contractors and subcontractors.

(34) (A) The company will have to give all unionized employees a pay raise.

Unions offer unionized workers a collective voice and bargaining power to negotiate improved salaries, benefits and working conditions.

According to the National Labor Relations Act, employees have the right to be a part of a union, and unions are given the autonomy to bargain and put forward their demands. Employers cannot disband these unions and must listen to the demands of their employees with recognition and consideration.

(35) (B) The same pay as the local workers in the foreign country.

The employee will be paid the same as the local workers since the pay structure will be based on the localization approach, which ensures that the employees are compensated based on the market rate of that particular position.

(36) (C) A cash bonus or raise.

Since monetary incentives are usually preferred over nonmonetary options, a cash bonus or a pay raise will be a suitable option in this scenario. A personalized note would be insufficient as the employee has shown real progress, but promotion would be a bit far-fetched at this level.

A small compensation would decrease the morale of the employee, and the motivation to excel might be lost. So, a raise in pay or a bonus is the most appropriate option.

(37) (C) Child support payments, tax debts and unpaid court fines.

Garnishments are court orders requiring an employer to deduct a portion of an employee's income or compensation and pay it straight to a creditor to fulfill a debt.

The employers are legally allowed to withhold some portion of the employee's salary and pay their debt to the state, whether it be legal or civilian, such as tax debts, court fines or child support. Personal debts such as memberships or loans are not included in this.

(38) (A) A federal law that forbids discrimination against 40-year-old or older employees/job applicants.

US citizens aged 40 and above are protected against discrimination in the workplace by the Age Discrimination in Employment Act.

According to this law, employers will not discriminate among individuals based on their age in any aspect of the job. From the interview to the benefits given to the workers, all employees will be treated equally.

(39) (C) A technique that ranks jobs based on their relevance or significance in the business.

The ranking technique is a method to assess jobs by placing them from most important to least.

Jobs are ranked depending on how essential they are and also ranked based on a set of features, such as ability, responsibility, knowledge and complexity.

(40) (A) Conduct a business pay practices poll.

By conducting a business pay practices poll, the fashion retailer can gather information and insights on the prevailing pay practices in the industry. This can help them understand the market rates, compensation trends, and benchmark their own compensation program against competitors. It provides valuable data that can inform the development of an effective and competitive compensation strategy.

(41) (B) A financial reward for promoting a particular number of items to each consumer.

Monetary rewards are usually preferred over nonmonetary ones.

Monetized incentives like bonuses provide workers the motivation to do the additional work needed to accomplish specific goals.

(42) (D) Depends on the outcomes sought.

Incentives are usually given when a new product is introduced or when an organization looks to achieve a specific goal in terms of target.

Providing incentives too often, especially monetary incentives, can be a burden on resources. Annual incentives to employees are not enough for the workers to maintain their determination toward achieving the goal.

An incentive, whether monetary or nonmonetary, should be given with a specific goal in mind for the betterment of the company. Randomly providing incentives to employees is counterproductive as the purpose behind the reward is lost.

(43) (B) A profit-sharing program that compensates employees based on the performance of the company.

A profit-sharing program is a type of pay plan in which a company gives its employees a share of its profits. By linking their pay to the company's profits, the program is meant to give employees a reason to work for the company's financial success.

No company can assure employment for all workers. Also, all staff members cannot be paid equally as they have different jobs which require unique skills.

The difference in pay demonstrates that some employees are at a higher level than others. Employee complaints are settled by HR, and it has nothing to do with the Scanlon plan.

(44) (C) Flexible work arrangements.

Flexible work arrangements fall under nonmonetary incentives and usually are a way to promote a better work-life balance. Health insurance policies and paid vacations are some other types of nonmonetary rewards that a company gives to its employees.

(45) (C) A strategy that gives salespeople a percentage of their total sales.

A commission-based plan is a way to pay employees where they get a percentage or a set amount for every sale or transaction. They give them a reason to sell more because their pay is directly linked to how well they do.

A commission plan does not include bonuses based on sales or the profit made off a sale. This plan also excludes the idea that the same amount of money be given to the salesperson after every sale as some sales are more of a success than others, and the money made from sales varies.

(46) (D) A strategy that provides employees a percentage of their salary based on how well they do their tasks.

An at-risk pay program is a type of performance-based pay plan in which workers are given a portion of the payment if they meet certain goals or targets. A large component of employees' pay is provided, and only some of it is withheld if the performance is not positive.

(47) (B) Ensuring performance appraisal and control.

HR management is centered around appraisal and performance management.

(48) (D) Both (B) and (C).

A performance appraisal can help to determine the functionality of employees over a defined period of time. It also allows companies to evaluate performance expectations and align work based on their organization's requirements.

(49) (D) All of the above.

Performance appraisal is a process for assessing a worker's performance against established goals or criteria. It is a tool for identifying the workers' development needs and training needs.

(50) (D) All of the above.

A performance appraisal will include a review of the employee's contribution to the company, a performance goal and an employee skill assessment. It also assesses the strengths and weaknesses of the employee.

(51) (A) Areas of improvement.

A performance appraisal helps employers identify areas of improvement in their processes.

(52) (D) All of the above.

Supervisors, managers and stakeholders (clients or investors) can perform a performance appraisal.

(53) (C) Provide feedback on employees' performance.

A performance appraisal helps identify the employees' performance over a set duration of time. It includes the skill assessment of the employees, the employees' performance objective and the employees' contribution to the organization.

(54) (C) A clear and objective set of criteria.

A performance appraisal is based on a clear and set objective of criteria. These objectives need to be solid factors, such as the employees' responsibilities, key performance indicators and behavioral indicators.

(55) (A) Standardized evaluation tools.

Bias can be eliminated from appraisal results by using a standard evaluation tool that can fairly judge the performance of all the employees in the company.

(56) (B) Annually or semiannually.

Performance appraisal is a process of evaluating an employee's performance against set goals or criteria. It can be conducted annually or semiannually.

(57) (D) Defining the company's vision.

Performance appraisals can help determine an employee's performance through interviews. The following steps are included in an appraisal process:

- Establish the standards around which performance will be judged.
- Make the employees aware of the standard.

- Measure employee performance.
- Compare performance to the set standards.
- Discuss appraisal with the employees.

(58) (C) Review and follow-up.

After collecting the data from the performance appraisal, the managers go through it to note down the employees' performance. The collected data is presented to the employees during the appraisal meetings.

(59) (D) Ongoing feedback.

After reviewing the work of an employee, the manager provides feedback. When the employee resubmits the work, the manager checks it and provides feedback again. This is an example of ongoing feedback.

(60) (B) Performance documentation.

When a manager or supervisor notes down employees' performance, it is known as performance documentation. This documentation is important and is discussed during the appraisal meeting.

(61) (A) An appraisal meeting.

The appraisal meeting is a meeting held between the supervisors and the employees in which the data collected from the appraisal is discussed.

The manager gives constructive criticism to the employees and helps them understand the areas in which they can improve.

(62) (A) Evaluating employee eligibility for promotions.

Performance documentation plays a crucial role in evaluating employee performance and determining their eligibility for promotions. It allows human resources to assess an employee's strengths, areas for improvement, and overall contribution to the organization. This documentation serves as a basis for making informed decisions regarding promotions and career advancement opportunities.

(63) (A) Recruiting top talent.

It is the responsibility of customized talent management to provide the employees with proper training and resources. They recruit top talent from a sea of employees, making sure to select the best-suited candidates for the job.

(64) (B) Halo effect.

When a recruiter is impressed by an employee and decides to ignore all other factors, they commit an error known as the halo effect.

(65) (A) The Civil Rights Act of 1964.

Title VII of the Civil Rights Act of 1964 states that no employee will be discriminated against based on race, religion, ethnicity, gender, religion, etc.

(66) (B) Be empathetic and understanding.

Managers need to be understanding and empathetic during an appraisal meeting. They need to help the employees understand the areas in which they lack. They must give constructive criticism to the employees and not blame them for their faults.

(67) (A) Total quality management.

Total quality management is the process by which a company's success is derived from its customer satisfaction. Performance appraisal is an important part of total quality management.

(68) (C) Central tendency bias.

Central tendency bias occurs when a recruiter marks all candidate scores as average regardless of performance.

(69) (A) The Fair and Accurate Credit Transactions Act.

The Fair and Accurate Credit Transactions Act is a federal law that regulates credit reports, among other things. It was passed in 2003 and amended the Fair Credit Reporting Act to provide consumers with greater control over their credit reports.

(70) (A) The Employee Polygraph Protection Act.

The Employee Polygraph Protection Act prohibits most private employers from using lie detector tests for pre-employment screening or during employment. The law was enacted in 1988 and applies to most employers in the private sector.

(71) (C) The Dodd-Frank Wall Street Reform and Consumer Protection Act.

The Dodd-Frank Wall Street Reform and Consumer Protection Act was passed in 2010 in order to promote financial stability within the United States and protect consumers from abusive financial deals.

The law also established new regulations for banks and other financial institutions and created the Consumer Financial Protection Bureau.

(72) (B) The Rehabilitation Act (1973).

The Rehabilitation Act of 1973 prohibits discrimination based on disability in work practices of the federal government and federal contractors. Federal contractors and federal agencies must take affirmative action to make use of and advance qualified individuals with disabilities.

(73) (D) All of the above.

In regard to the safety of an office, good management has an important role to play. Management must help create and implement a safety culture in the company, ensuring that workers are trained to identify and respond to potential threats. Part of this involves reviewing and evaluating the organization's security plan.

(74) (C) The Service Contract Act of 1965.

The Service Contract Act of 1965 offers minimum wages and fringe benefits, together with extra job conditions under service contracts. The law applies to nearly all contracts with the federal government and its contractors for services performed in the United States.

(75) (C) Collective bargaining.

Collective bargaining is the process of negotiation between a union and a company that represents its employees. The employees can negotiate better pay, benefits and working conditions with their employers by collective bargaining.

(76) (D) All of the above.

Unsafe working conditions can lead to accidents and injuries. Unsafe conditions can include using unsafe equipment, unsafe procedures around machines and improperly secured equipment.

(77) (A) OSHA makes guidelines for workplace safety and implements them.

The Occupational Health and Safety Administration is responsible for enforcing workplace safety standards.

(78) (A) A process in which representatives of employees and employers negotiate the employment terms and conditions of employment.

A collective bargaining process is where workers and employers work out terms and conditions of employment, including benefits such as salaries and working conditions.

(79) (D) All of the above.

A secure workplace is crucial for any company because it creates trust between management and workers, lowers costs for workers' compensation and enhances the reputation of the organization.

(80) (B) To determine whether the employees would like to be represented by a union.

The union drive and election process is created to allow the staff members to decide whether they would like to be represented by a union.

(81) (D) All of the above.

The supervisor's role in preventing accidents includes educating staff on office security policies and procedures, ensuring they exercise properly and adhere to established security protocols and motivating staff to report accidents or incidents.

(82) (B) The National Labor Relations Act.

The National Labor Relations Act guarantees the right of employees to take part in collective bargaining. It also helps to safeguard workers against reprisals for union activities.

(83) (D) All of the above.

Employers are able to reduce workplace accidents by preventing unsafe working conditions, training workers on how to run equipment safely and implementing safety protocols for unsafe work practices.

(84) (B) The National Labor Relations Act of 1935.

The National Labor Relations Act of 1935 banned yellow-dog contracts, where a worker agreed not to be associated with any labor union.

Likewise, the NLRA gave employees the right to develop and join unions and take part in collective bargaining.

(85) (A) The actions of a company to alter its basic elements.

Organizational change refers to the actions taken by a company to alter its fundamental components, such as the structure of its processes, solutions and culture.

Organizational change can also be triggered by internal or external factors and is generally needed for a company to remain competitive.

(86) (B) To avoid undesirable consequences, such as a company interruption and subsequent lost productivity.

The objective of a change management tactic is to steer clear of undesirable effects such as company disruptions and lost productivity.

(87) (B) A hands-on plan that ensures that a company can meet its important business duties in the event of an urgent situation.

If a company is in a state of emergency, enterprise continuity management is a plan that outlines procedures and controls to ensure that the company can continue to operate normally.

(88) (D) All of the above.

HR's role in ensuring business continuity includes creating and putting into practice business continuity strategies, providing guidelines and practices for workers' behavior when a disturbance occurs and giving employees disaster preparedness training.

(89) (D) All of the above.

Mergers and acquisitions are successful because they require large-scale organizational change, involve prompt and secure data integration and allow companies to create enormous value through synergies and economies of scale.

(90) (C) It is a crucial component for the prompt and secure integration of data.

Data integration is crucial for prompt and secure data integration in a successful merger or acquisition. It involves combining data from different sources and ensuring that the data is accurate, consistent and complete.

Proper data integration is essential for making informed business decisions and realizing the benefits of a merger or acquisition.

Test 4: Questions

(1) A company is conducting high-volume recruitment for a specific position. Which type of interview would be the best choice to ensure objectivity and reduce subjectivity during the interview process?

(A) Structured interview

(B) Unstructured interview

(C) Behavioral interview

(D) Informal interview

(2) Which of the following evaluation points do HR professionals use to score candidates during post-interview evaluations?

(A) Work experience, education and personality

(B) Specific questions associated with the project, prior experience and weak spots

(C) Cultural fit, communication skills and dress code

(D) Technical skills, language proficiency and teamwork abilities

(3) Why is data collection essential in HR metrics?

(A) It gives insights into the usefulness of recruitment plus talent management practices.

(B) It helps confirm the information provided by applicants during the job interview process.

(C) It helps create highly effective interviewing techniques and skills.

(D) It gives information about the project, the business and the culture of its candidates.

(4) Which stage in the job interview process entails scoring candidates on specific issues associated with the project, prior experience and weak spots?

(A) Conducting the interview

(B) Preparing for the interview

(C) Post-interview evaluations

(D) Developing interview questions

(5) Which interview type provides for a far more conversational and relaxed environment, offering insight into a candidate's personality, inspiration and communication skills?

(A) Structured interview

(B) Behavioral interview

(C) Unstructured interview

(D) Casual interview

(6) A manager rejects a job application since the applicant is overqualified for the placement.

What kind of interviewing error is the supervisor committing?

(A) Stereotyping and bias

(B) Halo/horn effect

(C) Attribution error

(D) Overconfidence

(7) What is a situational interview?

(A) An interview that assesses candidates' capacity to deal with particular issues they might encounter as they work for the business

(B) An interview that focuses on a candidate's experience and qualifications

(C) An interview that compares applicants according to their relative performance

(D) An interview that creates hiring choices based on a candidate's appearance

(8) What are important competencies that an interviewer should evaluate in a situational interview?

(A) Education, personality and appearance

(B) Problem-solving, decision-making and communication skills

(C) Age, gender and race

(D) Experience, skills and eligibility

(9) What type of questions do most interviewers ask in a situational interview?

(A) Closed-ended questions

(B) Questions that focus on clothing and appearance

(C) Open-ended questions

(D) Questions that aren't associated with the position

(10) A business is hiring for a customer service job, so the HR manager has a regular interview with five applicants.

During the job interview process, the interviewer can make comparisons between each candidate dependent on their responses. This is an example of __________.

(A) Candidate-order error

(B) Nonverbal behavior

(C) First impressions

(D) Impression management

(11) What is the distinction between a hierarchical structure and a uniform organization structure?

(A) A hierarchical organizational structure results in more rigid HR practices, while a uniform organizational structure results in more adaptable HR practices.

(B) Unlike a hierarchical organizational structure, a uniform organizational structure has an impact on the level of decision-making and authority.

(C) A simple organizational structure looks at workers at the same level, while a hierarchical structure deals with the whole business.

(D) None of the above.

(12) How do substance abuse screening tests help employers?

(A) Reduce the risk of accidents and injuries

(B) Improve employee health and wellness

(C) Lower absenteeism

(D) All of the above

(13) How can an organization ensure effective management of employee records?

(A) By keeping track of business records

(B) By ignoring the life cycle of records

(C) By not classifying and categorizing records

(D) By not maintaining the confidentiality of records

(14) Which of the following is not a best practice for effective employee records management?

(A) Maintaining record confidentiality

(B) Setting up a system to manage business records

(C) Classifying records based on content, format and purpose

(D) Disposing of records immediately after their creation

(15) What factors are not essential when it comes to monitoring HR systems?

(A) Headcounts

(B) Demographics

(C) Time-to-fill

(D) Number of social media followers

(16) By which method time elapses from when employees begin to achieve improved productivity?

(A) Time-to-hire

(B) Time-to-fill

(C) Acceptance rate

(D) Time-to-productivity

(17) Which of the following may a diminished approval rate indicate?

(A) The company offers competitive wages and benefits.

(B) The task is interesting.

(C) The business is effectively screening applicants.

(D) The company isn't supplying competitive benefits or salaries.

(18) What is controlled experimentation?

(A) A study strategy used in health care to evaluate the appearance of drugs

(B) A process for evaluating training programs

(C) A strategy used to collect feedback from the training participants

(D) A method for handling and tracking employee training

(19) What is the objective of a learning management system?

(A) To enhance the convenience of training courses

(B) To look at the outcome of training

(C) To gather responses from training participants

(D) To create and manage employee training courses

(20) Why are metrics utilized in development and training?

(A) To manage staff training

(B) To evaluate and assess the effectiveness of training

(C) To assess the delivery of training programs

(D) To identify areas that should be improved in the upcoming training efforts

(21) What is the purpose of questionnaires in training and participant surveys?

(A) To assess the usefulness of training programs

(B) To evaluate the result of the training on the organization

(C) To gather feedback from training personnel and identify improvement areas

(D) To assess the present knowledge, skills and abilities of the training participants

(22) What is pre-evaluation in the context of coaching assessment?

(A) An evaluation technique used to evaluate the convenience of a training program

(B) A procedure for evaluating the material and delivery of training courses

(C) An evaluation of the participants' current knowledge, skills and capabilities prior to the training program

(D) A review of what has been done very well, what can be improved and what lessons are learned after a program has been completed

(23) What is the objective of examinations in the context of coaching evaluation?

(A) To assess the participants' current knowledge, abilities and capabilities before the training program begins

(B) To assess the result of the organization's training efforts

(C) To establish areas for improvement within the upcoming training efforts

(D) To take a look at the appropriateness of the training course by assessing the participants' knowledge, abilities and skills before and after the class

(24) What's an after-action review?

(A) A research technique used to evaluate the appearance of drugs

(B) A process for evaluating the convenience of training courses

(C) A system to evaluate a training course, project and possibly other business initiatives

(D) A method for evaluating and managing employee training

(25) Which of the following isn't a stage in Lewin's Change Management Model?

(A) Unfreeze

(B) Change

(C) Empower

(D) Refreeze

(26) Kotter's Eight-Step Model for Change was created by ________.

(A) Kurt Lewin

(B) Prosci

(C) William Bridges

(D) John Kotter

(27) What does ADKAR stand for in the ADKAR Change Management Model?

(A) Awareness, Ability, Knowledge, Desire, Reinforcement

(B) Action, Accountability, Knowledge, Desire, Reinforcement

(C) Awareness, Adaptability, Knowledge, Drive, Resourcefulness

(D) Assessment, Adaptation, Knowledge, Drive, Reinforcement

(28) Which of the following is not a stage in the Kübler-Ross Change Curve?

(A) Denial

(B) Bargaining

(C) Acceptance

(D) Action

(29) What is the focus of the ADKAR Change Management Model?

(A) Changing the organization's culture

(B) Changing employee behavior

(C) Providing resources and tools to employees

(D) Minimizing resistance to change

(30) Who developed the Bridges Transition Model?

(A) Kurt Lewin

(B) John Kotter

(C) William Bridges

(D) Prosci

(31) Which stage of the Bridges Transition Model involves individuals processing the end of the current state and accepting that things are changing?

(A) Endings

(B) The Neutral Zone

(C) New Beginnings

(D) Transition

(32) John is an employee of a corporation with a pay-for-performance framework and has achieved his sales goals.

What kind of nonmonetary reward will John receive?

(A) A financial bonus for accomplishing the objectives

(B) Increased pay for his excellent performance

(C) A certificate of accomplishment

(D) A commission

(33) A company created a brand-new business plan focusing on innovation and creativity. The company's total rewards program comprises a starting salary, yearly incentives and health insurance, among other items.

Which of the following is a good example of the way the company's total rewards program may work?

(A) Giving individuals that have been effective for a long period a higher base salary

(B) Giving employees a health plan motivates them to live healthy lifestyles

(C) Giving annual bonuses depending on how well everyone did

(D) Starting a system that rewards staff members for thinking of new ideas and innovative means to fix issues

(34) What is a good example of procedural equity in a performance evaluation process?

(A) Friends of the supervisor get high-performance reviews regardless of performance

(B) A company's performance review procedure is transparent and applies specific criteria to all employees

(C) A manager gives a worker a bad performance grade with no suggestions or chances for improvement

(D) A manager rates a worker poorly based on individual bias rather than results

(35) What is a crucial aspect to think about when developing team incentives?

(A) The private functionality of team members

(B) How long the staff has been working together

(C) The team's main goals and targets

(D) The individual characteristics of the staff members

(36) What is unemployment insurance?

(A) A system that helps businesses with lost profits

(B) A program that helps workers who have lost their jobs

(C) A government program that helps workers who do not qualify for other government benefits

(D) A system that will help workers on strike

(37) Maria has been ill for a couple of days; therefore, she has not been able to work. She worries that if she takes excessive time off, she will not be able to pay her bills.

In this particular circumstance, what must Maria do?

(A) She must continue coming to work despite being ill.

(B) She must ask her employer for a leave of absence.

(C) She must use sick leave.

(D) She must ask her coworkers to fill in for her while she is gone.

(38) What are supplemental employee benefits?

(A) Benefits called for by law which most employers must offer

(B) Benefits a company offers on top of its standard benefits package

(C) Benefits provided to individuals doing work in certain fields

(D) Benefits offered to top executives and managers

(39) What is worker's compensation?

(A) A type of health insurance covering injuries or illnesses at work

(B) A program that helps people that are unemployed by offering them money

(C) A method that sets health and safety requirements for the workplace

(D) A reward for employees that have been with a company for a particular number of years and wish to retire

(40) A business has a pay policy that sets pay amounts depending on the typical pay of similar tasks in the labor market.

Which of the following pay policies determines this representation?

(A) Merit pay

(B) Market-based pay

(C) Seniority-based pay

(D) Performance-based pay

(41) A business pays its male workers a higher wage than the female employees for doing exactly the same task.

Which of the following is true?

(A) The Equal Pay Act has been implemented by the business.

(B) The business is violating the EPA.

(C) The distinction in pay may be clarified by the various levels of training.

(D) The distinction in pay may be clarified by job experience.

(42) What is the most significant advantage of using a computerized system to rate a job?

(A) It costs much less than the other techniques.

(B) It works faster.

(C) It gives more reliable results than other methods.

(D) It is easier to understand than some other methods.

(43) How does equity-based pay align with the interests of the company and the employees?

(A) It offers employees a higher salary as their base pay.

(B) It gives employees a sense of ownership in the company.

(C) It provides employees with more cash as a bonus.

(D) It provides much better coverage for health insurance.

(44) The board of directors at a multinational company should ___________.

(A) Make certain that managers are paid much less than executives

(B) Take a closer look at executive pay and set more rules about it

(C) Maintain secrecy about salaries

(D) Make sure that executives are paid much more than other employees

(45) An employee at an event planning business just registered for the company's life insurance.

Who will obtain the life insurance proceeds after the employee's death?

(A) The insurance company

(B) The designated beneficiary

(C) The employee's estate

(D) The employee's employer

(46) What is a cash balance plan?

(A) A program wherein participants get a particular sum upon retirement

(B) A medical insurance policy that reimburses policyholders for out-of-pocket costs

(C) A compensation program that issues workers other forms of payment

(D) A plan in which retirement benefits are presented as a cash balance

(47) Positive employee relations can be built by ___________.

(A) Discouraging communication

(B) Ensuring fair treatment

(C) Ignoring bullying and victimization

(D) Lack of promotions

(48) An ethical organization should __________.

(A) Have ethical guidelines

(B) Have open and transparent communication

(C) Report unethical behavior

(D) All of the above

(49) How can an ethical workplace environment be created?

(A) By ignoring an ethical behavior model

(B) By discouraging open-door policy

(C) By providing ethical training

(D) With a lack of communication

(50) Employee discipline can be managed by ____________.

(A) Establishing clear rules and expectations

(B) Creating employee policies

(C) Outlining proper conduct

(D) All of the above

(51) What does discipline in the workplace imply?

(A) That disciplinary actions should be gender biased

(B) That men should be dealt with harshly while handing out punishment

(C) That instances of harassment and discrimination should be addressed

(D) None of the above

(52) How can employee discipline be managed?

(A) By providing feedback

(B) By documenting incidents

(C) By using progressive discipline

(D) All of the above

(53) How does a company become the best company to work for?

(A) By making decisions independently without involving employees

(B) By developing employee recognition programs

(C) By prioritizing work over employees

(D) Both (A) and (C)

(54) What is the key to successful employee discipline?

(A) Approaching discipline as a constructive process

(B) Making the employees understand their behavior

(C) Maintaining employee confidentiality

(D) All of the above

(55) Good employee relations __________.

(A) Improve employee retention

(B) Lower absenteeism

(C) Improve employee morale

(D) All of the above

(56) Effective employee relations __________.

(A) Have no importance in business

(B) Don't affect an organization's success

(C) Are crucial for a positive workplace environment

(D) None of the above

(57) What can lead to a toxic workplace environment?

(A) Communication

(B) Bullying

(C) Gender equity

(D) Feedback

(58) How can HR acknowledge employee hard work?

(A) By providing a competitive salary

(B) By providing bonuses

(C) By providing recognition

(D) All of the above

(59) Poor employee relations can lead to ________.

(A) Lower turnover rates

(B) A negative workplace environment

(C) Increased productivity

(D) A successful organization

(60) Effective communication involves __________.

(A) Holding regular meetings

(B) Encouraging open conversation

(C) Supporting employees

(D) All of the above

(61) Employee rights include _____________.

(A) Fair treatment

(B) Protection of privacy

(C) Safe work environment

(D) All of the above

(62) What is progressive discipline?

(A) Suspending the employee on the first mistake

(B) Informally disciplining the employee

(C) Firing the employee

(D) Verbally warning the employee initially

(63) How can support be provided to struggling employees?

(A) By not taking their problems into account

(B) By ignoring their performance

(C) By arranging training sessions

(D) By describing their bad behavior

(64) Why is Google considered one of the best companies to work for?

(A) Google offers a creative environment.

(B) Google gives its employees flexible work schedules.

(C) Google offers childcare as well as other benefits.

(D) All of the above.

(65) How can a company increase employee retention?

(A) By maintaining a strict, goal-oriented work schedule

(B) By maintaining a toxic, competitive work environment

(C) By giving its employees attractive salary packages

(D) By aggressively correcting employee behavioral issues

(66) How can rules be enforced fairly in a workplace?

(A) By delaying disciplinary action

(B) By being inconsistent with rule enforcement

(C) By creating a gender bias while taking disciplinary action

(D) By holding the employees responsible for their actions

(67) Disciplining employees is the job of _________.

(A) HR

(B) The top management

(C) Supervisors

(D) None of the above

(68) What are employee relations?

(A) Relations between employees of different companies

(B) Relations between coworkers

(C) Relations between employees and the company they work for

(D) Relations between HR and the managing department

(69) What was the purpose of the Workforce Innovation and Opportunity Act of 2014?

(A) To establish minimum standards for work on federal contracts

(B) To improve services to disabled individuals

(C) To prohibit discrimination against individuals with disabilities in all areas of life

(D) To promote program coordination, key employment, education and training programs at all levels

(70) Which act established minimum standards for work on federal contracts?

(A) The Americans with Disability Act (ADA)

(B) The Walsh-Healey Act (1936)

(C) The Uniform Guidelines on Employee Selection Procedures (1978)

(D) The Drug-Free Workplace Act (1988)

(71) Which law prohibits discrimination based on pregnancy, childbirth or medical conditions related to pregnancy in employment?

(A) The Pregnancy Discrimination Act of 1978

(B) The Age Discrimination in Employment Act of 1967

(C) The Americans with Disability Act

(D) The Workforce Innovation and Opportunity Act of 2014

(72) What was the intent behind the Consolidated Omnibus Budget Reconciliation Act of 1986?

(A) To enable federal workers to manage, bargain collectively and also take part in labor organizations

(B) To offer help to employees and their families who may have lost their health benefits

(C) To protect employees and their communities by requiring companies to provide notice before covered plant closings and mass layoffs

(D) To preserve the safety of all workers, clients and the public

(73) What is the intent behind the Older Workers Benefit Protection Act of 1990?

(A) To protect employees and their communities by requiring companies to provide notice before covered plant closings and mass layoffs

(B) To provide more mature workers benefits equal to those offered to young workers

(C) To create minimum standards for work on federal contracts

(D) To grow the scope of civil rights

(74) What was the main function of the Civil Service Reform Act of 1978?

(A) To provide federal managers flexibility to enhance government operations and efficiency while protecting workers from unfair practices

(B) To enable investigators to collect information when looking into terrorism-related crimes

(C) To govern the compilation, use, maintenance and dissemination of individualized information maintained in federal agencies' records

(D) To enable federal workers to manage, bargain collectively and take part in labor organizations

(75) What is good faith in labor relations?

(A) A concept where just the union acts honestly and sincerely

(B) A concept where both employers and the union act sincerely

(C) A concept in which the employer acts honestly and sincerely

(D) A concept in which the union acts sincerely and the employer acts dishonestly

(76) Which of the following is a guideline for workers who go on strike?

(A) Using physical threats or force

(B) Treating replacement workers unfairly

(C) Respecting property rights

(D) All of the above

(77) What is a contract agreement?

(A) A nonbinding document between the union and the employer

(B) A legally binding document between the employer and the union

(C) A document that covers just hours and wages

(D) A booklet that isn't subject to federal and state labor laws

(78) What are grievances in labor relations?

(A) Complaints raised by companies about working conditions

(B) Complaints raised by employees about working conditions

(C) Complaints raised by the union about benefits and wages

(D) Complaints raised by the authorities about labor laws

(79) Which of the following are guidelines for managing grievances?

(A) Being timely, professional and respectful in all communications

(B) Thoroughly documenting all measures in the process

(C) Making choices based on biases and assumptions

(D) All of the above

(80) What is the purpose of safety evaluations in the workplace?

(A) To determine unsafe conditions along with potential hazards

(B) To increase productivity and reduce costs

(C) To reduce employee pay

(D) To reduce vacation time

(81) What is an example of PPE?

(A) A fire extinguisher

(B) Carpet cleaner

(C) Hard hat

(D) Desk lamp

(82) How can an employer reduce stress in the office?

(A) By implementing a work-life balance

(B) By implementing a dress code

(C) By increasing the workload

(D) By reducing vacation time

(83) What is a likely result of workplace smoking?

(A) Increased productivity

(B) Improved respiratory health

(C) Increased cardiovascular disease

(D) Improved physical fitness

(84) What are immediate circumstances that could negatively influence business functions?

(A) Workplace violence

(B) Natural disasters

(C) Changes in company culture

(D) Pandemics

(85) What is the aim of a risk assessment?

(A) To assess the likelihood of a terrorist attack on the United States as well as the possible impact on businesses and employees

(B) To measure the possibility of a fire and its possible effect on employees and businesses

(C) To assess the likelihood of an earthquake and the possible effect on people and businesses

(D) To assess the chance of tornadoes and the possible effect on employees and businesses

(86) A business wants to improve workplace security. It undertook a risk assessment and later determined that it must put in physical security measures.

Which of the following is a good example of a security measure?

(A) Conducting a security audit

(B) Training employees on how to understand suspicious behavior

(C) Installing security cameras

(D) Developing an emergency response plan

(87) An employer encourages risk-free workplace behavior by establishing specific security policies and setting safety goals.

What is this an example of?

(A) Increasing supervisor support

(B) Conducting operational safety reviews

(C) Reducing unsafe acts

(D) Using personal protective equipment

(88) What is the maximum time frame for reporting severe injuries and fatalities to OSHA?

(A) 15 days

(B) 30 days

(C) 60 days

(D) 90 days

(89) What is the primary reason for installing mechanical security systems in the workplace?

(A) To reduce the spread of infectious diseases

(B) To prevent cyberattacks

(C) To protect against potential threats

(D) To promote employee health

(90) An employee removes a safety guard to clean a machine but forgets to unplug it. He is at risk of injury if the machine is accidentally activated.

Which of the following best describes the situation?

(A) Improperly guarded equipment

(B) Defective equipment

(C) Hazardous procedures around machines

(D) Improper illumination

Test 4: Answers & Explanations

(1) (A) Structured interview.

Structured interviews are good for high-volume recruitment tasks since they include a set of fixed questions that are regularly evaluated for all applicants.

This ensures objectivity and reduces subjectivity during the job interview process, as all applicants are examined in the same way.

(2) (B) Specific questions associated with the project, prior experience and weak spots.

HR professionals score candidates on specific issues associated with the project, prior experience in the field, determination and any weaknesses or drawbacks that have been noticed during the job interview.

These scores are then set alongside the scores of various other applicants to determine the ideal match for the position.

(3) (A) It gives insights into the usefulness of recruitment plus talent management practices.

By gathering and analyzing information, HR professionals are able to gauge the results of the HR methods and make educated choices to enhance them.

(4) (C) Post-interview evaluations.

Post-interview evaluations call for scoring candidates on specific issues associated with the project, prior experience in the field, determination and any weaknesses or drawbacks noticed during the job interview.

(5) (C) Unstructured interview.

In an unstructured interview, the interviewer doesn't comply with predetermined questions, making it possible for the employment interview to run more conversationally.

These kinds of interviews are done in a casual atmosphere, providing the interviewer with more insight into a candidate's personality, inspiration and communication skills.

Open-ended questions are usually used to enable candidates to showcase their qualities and skills in a more natural environment.

(6) (A) Stereotyping and bias.

The manager can make assumptions about the applicants based on their qualifications instead of evaluating their fit for the job requirements. This particular error is a kind of stereotyping and bias.

(7) (A) An interview that assesses a candidate's capacity to deal with particular issues they might encounter as they work for the business.

A structured situational interview seeks to evaluate a candidate's capacity to handle particular issues encountered while working for the business.

(8) (B) Problem-solving, decision-making and communication skills.

The crucial competencies that an interviewer should wish to evaluate in a situational interview are problem-solving, teamwork, communication skills, decision-making and dealing with challenging situations.

(9) (C) Open-ended questions.

In a situational interview, interviewers should ask open-ended questions that permit the person to offer a comprehensive response. Open-ended questions often generate much more information from the applicant, resulting in a more extensive understanding of the candidate's experience, skills and capabilities.

Open-ended questions encourage applicants to make a more comprehensive and nuanced response. These questions aren't restricted to a certain answer and allow the person to expand on qualifications, skills and experiences. This can assist interviewers in acquiring insight into the candidate's thought process, communication style and problem-solving skills.

(10) (A) Candidate-order error.

The scenario described is referred to as candidate-order error. It happens when the interviewer compares each subsequent person to the prior one and decides based on relative performance rather than complete performance.

To avoid this, it's crucial for interviewers to assess each applicant on their merit and not make comparisons between candidates.

(11) (A) A hierarchical organizational structure results in more rigid HR practices, while a uniform organizational structure results in more adaptable HR practices.

An organization's structure impacts the amount of authority and decision-making ability of HR professionals. A flat organizational structure with decentralized decision-making can lead to more flexible and responsive HR practices. In contrast, a hierarchical structure can lead to more inflexible and bureaucratic HR practices.

(12) (D) All of the above.

Drug abuse screening tests can assist companies in various ways, including ensuring a productive and safe place of work, lowering the danger of injuries and accidents, enhancing employee well-being, reducing absenteeism and boosting efficiency.

(13) (A) By keeping track of business records.

To ensure effective management of employee records, an organization must keep track of business records, including creating, using, storing and disposing of them. The system should be designed to meet the organization's specific needs.

Option B is incorrect because ignoring the life cycle of records can lead to mismanagement, loss of data and regulatory noncompliance.

Option C is incorrect because classifying and categorizing records helps organizations manage their records more effectively and makes it easier to locate specific records when needed.

Option D is incorrect because maintaining record confidentiality is crucial, and any conscious or unconscious leak should be looked into immediately so that information regarding the employees can remain private.

(14) (D) Disposing of records immediately after their creation.

Disposing of records immediately after their creation is not a best practice for effective employee records management. Rather, the records' life cycle should be documented and followed to ensure they are managed effectively.

(15) (D) Number of social media followers.

The number of individual social media followers isn't an important information point to observe using HR systems. Rather, businesses must track data points such as time-to-fill, demographics and headcount to produce data-driven choices and enhance HR processes.

(16) (D) Time-to-productivity.

Time-to-productivity measures the time elapsed from when employees begin work to when they achieve increased productivity. It is able to offer useful insights into the onboarding process's success and the effect of employee training and development programs.

(17) (D) The company isn't supplying competitive benefits or salaries.

A low acceptance rate could indicate the organization isn't offering competitive benefits or salaries or the work is undesirable.

(18) (B) A process for evaluating training programs.

Controlled testing is a research technique utilized to look at the usefulness of training programs. This method randomly assigns individuals to an experimental group that gets the training plan, along with a control group that doesn't.

The results of both groups then decide whether the training program had a positive impact. This process allows trainers to objectively determine the program's effectiveness and make data-driven choices to boost future training efforts.

(19) (D) To create and manage employee training courses.

The goal of a learning management system is to create and manage employee education courses.

An LMS offers a centralized platform for businesses to manage, deliver and observe their training programs. It allows coaches to develop and publish course material, assign courses to workers, track employee improvement and completion and produce reports on instruction effectiveness.

(20) (B) To evaluate and assess the effectiveness of training.

Metrics are utilized to track training effectiveness and assess learning. Metrics are measurable data points that assist coaches in knowing how well their training programs are meeting their objectives and goals.

They can consist of completion rates, pass rates, assessment scores, employee performance information and participant responses. Trainers are able to utilize this data to identify weaknesses and strengths in their training programs and make data-driven decisions to enhance them.

(21) (C) To gather feedback from training personnel and identify improvement areas.

The goal of participant surveys and questionnaires in training is to gather responses from individuals and determine areas for improvement.

These tools allow trainers to collect responses from individuals about the usefulness of the instruction, the caliber of the training materials, the effectiveness of the instructor, along with various other facets of the training plan. This feedback can be utilized to enhance future training efforts by identifying areas for development and addressing participant concerns.

(22) (C) An evaluation of the participants' current knowledge, skills and capabilities prior to the training program.

Pretesting offers coaches a baseline of the participants' knowledge, abilities and capabilities before the training plan starts. Trainers are able to utilize this information to design programs that are customized to the participants' objectives and needs.

(23) (D) To take a look at the training course by assessing the participants' knowledge, abilities and skills before and after the class.

Post-testing provides coaches with information regarding the usefulness of the training programs by looking at the participants' abilities, capabilities and capabilities before and after the training course. This information can be used to spot areas of development and make data-driven choices to enhance training efforts in the future.

(24) (C) A system to evaluate a training course, project and possibly other business initiatives.

An After-Action Review is a method to assess and evaluate a training program, project or other business initiative.

AAR reflects on the team's performance, identifies challenges and positive results and makes recommendations for improvement in the long term. This involves collecting feedback from team members as well as stakeholders and analyzing the information to determine areas for improvement.

(25) (C) Empower.

Empowerment isn't a stage in Lewin's Change Management Model. The three phases of Lewin's Change Management Model are unfreeze, refreeze and change.

(26) (D) John Kotter.

John Kotter created Kotter's Eight-Step Model for Change. This particular design is meant to assist organizations in managing change efficiently by offering a structured approach.

(27) (A) Awareness, Ability, Knowledge, Desire, Reinforcement.

ADKAR stands for Awareness, Ability, Knowledge, Desire and Reinforcement. This model is a goal-oriented change management framework that focuses on assisting individuals and organizations to achieve particular outcomes.

(28) (D) Action.

Action is not a stage in the Kübler-Ross Change Curve. The five phases of the curve are denial, depression, bargaining, anger and validation.

(29) (B) Changing employee behavior.

The emphasis of the ADKAR Change Management Model is changing employee behavior. The model identifies the crucial stages people undergo whenever they experience change and gives a framework for handling these stages effectively.

It is meant to assist organizations in achieving their goals by ensuring that workers adopt the desired actions and practices essential for good results.

(30) (C) William Bridges.

William Bridges designed the Bridges Transition Model. This model focuses on the psychological and emotional facets of change and offers a structured method of controlling the transition process.

(31) (A) Endings.

At this stage, individuals begin to recognize that the current state is coming to an end and start to let go of old behaviors, attitudes and relationships. They may experience a range of emotions, including sadness, anger and fear, as they come to terms with the changes that are occurring.

(32) (C) A certificate of accomplishment.

A certificate acknowledging John's achievement, though nonmonetary, could be proudly displayed in his workplace. A bonus or a commission can be a monetary benefit.

Nonmonetary incentives consist of paid holidays, badges, flexible working hours and so on. A pay increase also is a monetary advantage.

(33) (D) Starting a system that rewards staff members for thinking of new ideas and innovative means to fix issues.

The firm's brand-new business approach concentrates on innovation and innovation; hence, a recognition system that recognizes staff members for their innovative solutions and ideas could align with the incentives program.

(34) (B) A company's performance review procedure is transparent and applies specific criteria to all employees.

Procedural equity in performance evaluation means fairness and consistency for all employees. This should be the case with all performance evaluations. There should be no personal bias when assessing an employee, and no benefits should be given to people who are acquaintances.

Employers should not hold personal grudges and must give employees opportunities to improve.

(35) (C) The team's main goals and targets.

When creating team incentives, it's essential to consider the team's overall goals and objectives to ensure team members are motivated to work together toward a common goal.

An individual member's performance is less important than the team's overall performance since the incentives are meant to get the team to work together instead of competing.

(36) (B) A program that helps workers who have lost their jobs.

The goal of the unemployment insurance program is to financially help those who have lost their jobs through no fault of their own. The financial help is temporary until another company hires the employee.

This program does not give money to companies that have experienced a profit loss due to a slowdown in business. This program does not help workers on strike as these workers choose not to work.

(37) (C) She must use sick leave.

If Maria's employer gives employees sick leave, the best thing for her to do in this situation would be to use it to take time off work to get better.

Working while sick is difficult and uncomfortable. It affects health as well as work performance. A leave of absence implies that she is absent for other personal reasons, and some companies do not give paid leaves.

Helping a colleague is a good deed, but a single person cannot do multiple tasks in an office where work is already divided among employees. So, sick leave is the most appropriate answer in this situation.

(38) (B) Benefits a company offers on top of its standard benefits package.

Supplemental employee benefits like disability insurance, life insurance, retirement plans and wellness programs are meant to give employees more financial protection, security and support.

Benefits are given to a company's employees based on the organization's resources and market approach. Not all firms can give supplemental benefits. These benefits are given to deserving employees when they achieve certain goals.

(39) (A) A type of health insurance covering injuries or illnesses at work.

Worker's compensation is meant to help employees who can't work because of an illness or injury by giving them money and medical care. It is unemployment insurance that makes sure that temporarily unemployed individuals are given money for their basic needs.

The retirement plan includes employees who have been with the company for some time and want to retire.

The Workplace Safety Act is responsible for establishing a safe workplace environment for workers.

(40) (B) Market-based pay.

Market-based pay is a policy that sets pay levels based on what similar jobs in the outside labor market are paid.

Other types of pay include seniority-based pay, where employees' pay increases as they spend more years with the company. Performance-based pay is based on an employee's performance. Sometimes a portion of the payment is withheld in case of unsatisfactory performance.

Merit pay is an incentive pay, like a bonus or a promotion, given when an employee performs a task well.

(41) (B) The business is violating the EPA.

The Equal Pay Act states that people with similar jobs requiring the same skill set and knowledge are paid the same wage.

Under this act, employers are not allowed to discriminate pay based on sex, culture, race, religion and age. The difference in pay can only be based on the employee's job position, not on previous work experience or education.

(42) (C) It gives more reliable results than other methods.

A computerized way to evaluate a job is more accurate than others because it doesn't depend on human error or bias.

Personal bias in a workplace is prohibited in any circumstance, so the computerized rating of jobs is introduced to remove this. It is not as cost-effective as manual evaluation and is not easier than the human method.

Computerized rating of jobs is just as time-consuming as a manual job rating.

(43) (B) It gives employees a sense of ownership in the company.

When employees have a stake in the company, they are more likely to work harder and make good decisions. It is a form of non-cash compensation. Employees have stock appreciation rights and partake in the ownership of the firm. This equity-based pay does not give more salary to employees or extra bonuses.

(44) (B) Take a closer look at executive pay and set more rules about it

The board of directors, specifically the compensation committee, should regularly review and set compensation packages for executives, ensuring they are fair, competitive, and aligned with the company's objectives. This includes base salary, bonuses, equity, and other benefits. This scrutiny is important for maintaining trust with shareholders, employees, and the public, and for ensuring the long-term success of the company.

(45) (B) The designated beneficiary.

The employee's specified beneficiary will get the life insurance proceeds in the case of their death. The purpose of the insurance plan is that the employee's family or beneficiaries get the money the employee put aside.

(46) (D) A plan in which retirement benefits are presented as a cash balance.

Each employee in a cash balance plan has an individual account to which their employer contributes a predetermined annual proportion of their salary.

Upon retirement, the employee's account amount is multiplied by an interest rate to determine the payout. The health insurance policy pays medical bills or hospital admissions and medications.

A monetary compensation scheme issues checks to employees when they accomplish a certain goal.

(47) (B) Ensuring fair treatment.

Taking care of the rights of the employees is known as fair treatment. Fair treatment can directly improve employee relations.

Accommodation for disabled employees, financial compensation and benefits, vacation and paid-off days are some examples of fair workplace treatment.

(48) (D) All of the above.

An organization should have ethical guidelines, open and transparent communication and report all kinds of unethical behavior. These help the organization treat its employees fairly and create a healthy work environment.

(49) (C) By providing ethical training.

An ethical workplace can be created by providing ethical training to employees. Teaching the employees to make the right decisions can help the organization create an ethical environment. These programs also help build moral intuition and good decision-making ability.

(50) (D) All of the above.

Employee discipline is important for making sure that an employee is proving to be a valuable member of the organization. It can be maintained by establishing clear rules and expectations, creating employee policies and publishing manuals that outline proper ethical conduct.

(51) (C) That instances of harassment and discrimination should be addressed.

Cases of misconduct and ill-discipline should be reported accordingly.

(52) (D) All of the above.

Employee discipline can be maintained by establishing clear rules and expectations, creating employee policies and publishing manuals that outline proper ethical conduct.

(53) (B) By developing employee recognition programs.

Employee recognition plans are ways deserving employees are identified in an organization. Employees are often rewarded with gift cards, promotions, paid vacations and other incentives.

These programs are made so that the employees feel connected to their company while the company retains talent.

(54) (D) All of the above.

Employer self-discipline involves specific expectations and rules, developing employee policies, as well distributing manuals that outline correct ethical behavior. Additionally, incidents of poor judgment and ill discipline must be reported appropriately.

(55) (D) All of the above.

Great employee relationships increase employee retention, decrease absenteeism and boost employee morale.

(56) (C) Are crucial for a positive workplace environment.

Great employee relationships are created when a business develops a beneficial connection because of its workers.

(57) (B) Bullying.

A toxic environment is created when bullying ensues in the workplace. Behaviors associated with humiliating or ridiculing employees lead to bullying.

Many types of bullying may occur in any workplace, such as physical bullying, cyberbullying or psychological bullying.

(58) (D) All of the above.

There are many ways for an organization to acknowledge its employees. Some of these include rewards in the form of gift cards, promotions, paid vacations and other celebrations.

(59) (B) A negative workplace environment.

Effective employee relations are built when an organization maintains a positive relationship with its employees. Similarly, bad employee relations led to a negative working environment.

(60) (D) All of the above.

Communication in the workplace helps employees express their thoughts effectively and makes them feel cared for and valued by the organization.

The organization can maintain good communication by holding regular meetings, encouraging open conversation and supporting employees.

(61) (D) All of the above.

Employees put in hard work and effort to help a company meet its goals.

The organization should treat them fairly, respect their privacy and provide a safe working environment.

(62) (D) Verbally warning the employee initially.

The first step of progressive discipline is to verbally warn the employee.

The second step is to inform them by issuing a written warning. The third and fourth steps include suspension and termination, respectively. This helps the organization rectify issues in the first few stages of misconduct.

(63) (C) By arranging training and sessions.

The company can arrange training sessions for struggling employees to help them get on track as soon as possible.

An organization can also support its employees by providing them with timely feedback about their work, coaching them in problem areas for the employees, etc.

(64) (D) All of the above.

Google is considered the best company to work for because it values its employees. It offers a creative environment to the employees, the employees have flexible work schedules and they are provided alternative work arrangements and family-friendly policies like childcare and other benefits.

(65) (C) By giving its employees attractive salary packages.

Employee retention is the rate of employees recruited into the company and their sustainability.

A company can increase employee retention by appreciating good employees, rewarding them for their hard work and success, offering them different training programs that focus on their growth and providing them flexibility in work schedules, vacations and salary.

(66) (D) By holding the employees responsible for their actions.

Employee discipline is important for making sure that an employee is proving to be a valuable member of the organization.

(67) (A) HR.

HR is responsible for maintaining employee discipline. They can orient employees on the code of conduct, punish violators and issue disciplinary actions.

(68) (C) Relations between employees and the company they work for.

The relationship the employees have with their organization is known as employee relations. Effective employee relations are built when an organization maintains a positive relationship with its employees.

(69) (D) To promote program coordination, key employment, education and training programs at all levels.

The Workforce Innovation and Opportunity Act of 2014 was enacted to promote program coordination, key employment, education and training programs at all levels, including federal, state and local levels, to improve employment, education and training outcomes for individuals, particularly those with barriers to employment.

It aims to increase access to and opportunities for employment, education, training and support services for individuals seeking to enter or re-enter the labor force, including those with disabilities, youth and individuals with limited English proficiency.

(70) (B) The Walsh-Healey Act (1936).

The Walsh-Healey Act established minimum standards for work on federal contracts. It requires contractors to pay workers a minimum wage, keep certain documents and comply with specific health and safety requirements.

(71) (A) The Pregnancy Discrimination Act of 1978.

The Pregnancy Discrimination Act prohibits discrimination in employment based on pregnancy, childbirth or health conditions associated with pregnancy. It requires companies to treat pregnancy-related conditions just like other health conditions.

(72) (B) To offer help to employees and their families who may have lost their health benefits.

The Consolidated Omnibus Budget Reconciliation Act of 1986 provides employees and their families that have lost their health benefits the right to decide to continue with their health benefits for a set length of time. It applies to employers with 20 or maybe more employees.

(73) (B) To provide more mature workers benefits equal to those offered to young workers.

The Older Workers Benefit Protection Act of 1990 amended the Age Discrimination in Employment Act of 1967 and also provided extra protections for more mature workers.

It requires companies to provide more mature workers benefits equal to those offered to young workers.

(74) (A) To provide federal managers flexibility to enhance government operations and efficiency while protecting workers from unfair practices.

The Civil Service Reform Act of 1978 aimed to offer federal managers flexibility to enhance government operations and efficiency while protecting workers from unfair practices. It established brand-new rules for federal personnel management, which included collective bargaining and dispute resolution procedures.

(75) (B) A concept where both employer and union act sincerely.

Good faith in labor relations is a concept where both employer and union act sincerely and honestly. It requires parties to come to the bargaining table with an honest intent to reach an agreement, to bargain in good faith and to make every reasonable effort to reach a mutually acceptable agreement.

(76) (C) Respecting property rights.

Some key strike guidelines include respecting property rights, refraining from using physical force or threats and treating replacement workers fairly. These guidelines help ensure strikes are conducted peacefully and lawfully.

(77) (B) A legally binding document between the employer and the union.

A contract agreement is a legally binding document between the employer and the union. It covers various topics, including wages, hours, benefits and working conditions. The agreement is subject to federal and state labor laws.

(78) (B) Complaints raised by employees about working conditions.

Grievances are common workplace complaints that workers make regarding their work conditions. They can cover issues including working conditions, wages, hours, benefits and other items. Ideally, employers will have a grievance procedure in place to handle these complaints.

(79) (A) Being timely, professional and respectful in all communications.

The guidelines for handling grievances include being timely, respectful and professional in all communications, thoroughly documenting all steps of the process and making decisions based on facts and information, not on conceits or biases.

(80) (A) To determine unsafe conditions along with potential hazards.

Performing safety reviews is one way that employers can determine possible hazards and unsafe conditions in the workplace.

(81) (C) Hard hat.

A hard hat is one type of personal protective equipment. PPE protects workers from injuries due to falling objects, electrical currents or contact with harsh chemicals, among other things.

(82) (A) By implementing a work-life balance.

One way that employers can reduce stress is to promote a better work-life balance. This requires providing flexible work hours, family and personal time off, and encouraging workers to take breaks and vacations.

(83) (C) Increased cardiovascular disease.

Smoking in the workplace can lead to severe health effects, such as cardiovascular disease, lung cancer and respiratory issues. It does not improve fitness, respiratory health or productivity.

(84) (C) Changes in company culture.

An emergency can occur at any time, such as pandemics, workplace violence, natural disasters or any other situation that stops an organization from functioning normally.

Changes in the company culture are not considered emergencies that could adversely affect other functions or business services.

(85) (A) To assess the likelihood of a terrorist attack on the United States as well as the possible impact on businesses and employees.

A risk assessment aims to assess the likelihood of a terrorist attack and its potential impact on employees and businesses. Risk assessments help employers identify potential threats and mitigate them.

(86) (C) Installing security cameras.

Physical security measures are designed to limit access to a building or facility. Some examples include security cameras, access control systems and barriers like fences.

Conducting a security audit, training employees and developing an emergency response plan are important steps in securing the workplace but aren't examples of physical security measures.

(87) (C) Reducing unsafe acts.

The question describes an employer encouraging safe behavior in the workplace by establishing clear safety policies and setting safety goals, which is an example of reducing unsafe acts.

Increasing supervisor support, conducting operational safety reviews and using PPE aren't ways to encourage safe workplace behavior. They're safety policies the employer has implemented.

(88) (D) 90 days.

Employers have to report severe injuries and fatalities sustained by their employees to OSHA within a maximum of 90 days. This ensures OSHA can investigate the incident and take the necessary steps to prevent similar incidents in the future.

An employer who fails to report severe employee injuries may face fines or citations.

(89) (C) To protect against potential threats.

The primary reason for installing mechanical security systems in the workplace is to protect against potential threats.

Mechanical security systems, such as access control systems, video surveillance systems and alarms, can help deter potential intruders and provide an added layer of protection for employees and property.

(90) (C) Hazardous procedures around machines.

While the employee has removed the safety guard to clean the machine, he hasn't unplugged it. This could lead to an injury if the machine is accidentally activated.

Made in the USA
Coppell, TX
13 March 2024